8

Selected Poems

Selected
Poems

1957–1987

W.D. Snodgrass

Many of the poems in this volume have been previously published in books, periodicals, broadsides and the like, some in different form. By kind permission, they are reprinted here from:

Heart's Needle, published by Alfred A. Knopf, Inc., 1959.

Remains, Perishable Press, 1970.

Remains: A Sequence of Poems copyright © 1985 by W. D. Snodgrass, reprinted with the permission of BOA Editions, Ltd.

The Boy Made of Meat, published by William Ewert, 1982.

After Experience, Harper & Row, Publishers, Inc., 1967; and Oxford University Press, 1968.

Memphis State Review, in which "Manet: 'The Execution of the Emperor Maximilian'" appeared.

The Fuehrer Bunker: A Cycle of Poems in Progress, copyright © 1977 by W. D. Snodgrass, reprinted with the permission of BOA Editions, Ltd. Poems from "The Fuehrer Bunker" have also appeared in editions published in 1983 by Palaemon Press and Pterodactyl Press, as well as *American Poetry Review* (January–February, 1977), *The Kenyon Review,* New Series, Fall '79 (I.4), and *Salmagundi.*

If Birds Build with Your Hair, published by Nadja Press, 1979, and by Derry Press.

A Locked House published by William Ewert, 1986, and *The Syracuse Scholar,* 1983. "Old Jewelry" was published by Palaemon Press, and by *Stand.* "D. D. Byrde Calling Jennie Wrenne" was published by William Ewert in 1984. "A Valediction," "Silver Poplars," and "The Last Time" appeared in *Ploughshares* (July 1982).

Kinder Capers, three poems published by Nadja Press, 1986. Portions of "The Death of Cock Robin" appeared in *American Poetry Review* (January–February, 1987), *The Kenyon Review,* New Series, Spring '85 (VII:2), *New York Quarterly,* Summer, 1985, *Negative Capability, Salmagundi, Graham House Review, New Virginia Review,* and *Scarab.*

Library of Congress Cataloging-in-Publication Data

Snodgrass, W. D. (William De Witt), 1926–
Selected poems, 1957–1987.

I. Title.
PS3537.N32A6   1987   811'.54   87–9463
ISBN 0–939149–61–3

For Kathy
who puts things together

Contents

Heart's Needle

Ten Days Leave

He steps down from the dark train, blinking; stares
At trees like miracles. He will play games
With boys or sit up all night touching chairs.
Talking with friends, he can recall their names.

Noon burns against his eyelids, but he lies
Hunched in his blankets; he is half awake
But still lacks nerve to open up his eyes;
Supposing it were just his old mistake?

But no; it seems just like it seemed. His folks
Pursue their lives like toy trains on a track.
He can foresee each of his father's jokes
Like words in some old movie that's come back.

He is like days when you've gone some place new
To deal with certain strangers, though you never
Escape the sense in everything you do,
"We've done this all once. Have I been here, ever?"

But no; he thinks it must recall some old film, lit
By lives you want to touch; as if he'd slept
And must have dreamed this setting, peopled it,
And wakened out of it. But someone's kept

His dream asleep here like a small homestead
Preserved long past its time in memory
Of some great man who lived here and is dead.
They have restored his landscape faithfully:

The hills, the little houses, the costumes:
How real it seems! But he comes, wide awake,
A tourist whispering through the priceless rooms
Who must not touch things or his hand might break

Their sleep and black them out. He wonders when
He'll grow into his sleep so sound again.

At the Park Dance

As the melting park
darkens, the firefly winks
to signal loving strangers
from their pavilion
lined with Easter colored
lights, fading out together

until they merge with
weathered huge trees and join
the small frogs, those warm singers;
and they have achieved
love's vanishing point
where all perspectives mingle,

where even the most
close things are indistinct
or lost, where bright worlds shrink,
they will grope to find
blind eyes make all one world;
their unseen arms, horizons.

Beyond, jagged stars
are glinting like jacks hurled
farther than eyes can gather;
on the dancefloor, girls
turn, vague as milkweed floats
bobbing from childish fingers.

Orpheus

Stone lips to the unspoken cave;
Fingering the nervous strings, alone,
I crossed that gray sill, raised my head
To lift my song into the grave
Meanders of unfolding stone,
Following where the echo led
Down blind alleys of our dead.

Down the forbidden, backward street
To the lower town, condemned, asleep
In blank remembering mazes where
Smoke rose, the ashes hid my feet
And slow walls crumpled, settling deep
In rubble of the central square.
All ruin I could sound was there.

At the charred rail and windowsill,
Widows hunched in fusty shawls,
This only once the Furies wept;
The watchdog turned to hear me till
Head by head forgot its howls,
Loosed the torn images it kept,
Let sag its sore jaws and slept.

Then to my singing's radius
Seethed faces like a pauper's crowd
Or flies of an old injury.
The piteous dead who lived on us
Whined in my air, anarchic, loud
Till my soft voice that set them free,
Lost in this grievous enemy,

Rose up and laid them in low slumbers;
I meant to see in them what dark
Powers be, what eminent plotters.
Midmost those hushed, downcast numbers
Starved Tantalus stood upright, stark,
Waistdeep where the declining waters
Swelled their tides, where Danaus' daughters

Dropped in full surf their unfilled tub;
Now leaned against his rolling stone
Slept Sisyphus beneath the hill;
That screaming half-beast, strapped at the hub,
Whom Juno's animal mist had known,
Ixion's wheel creaked and was still.
I held all hell to hear my will.

"Powers of the Underworld, who rule
All higher powers by graft or debt,
Within whose mortgage all men live:
No spy, no shining power's fool,
I think in the unthought worlds to get
The light you only freely give
Who are all bright worlds' negative.

You gave wink in an undue crime
To love—strong even here, they say.
I sing, as the blind beggars sing,
To ask of you this little time
—All lives foreclose in their due day—
That flowered bride cut down in Spring,
Struck by the snake, your underling."

In one long avenue she was
Wandering toward me, vague, uncertain,
Limping a little still, the hair
And garments tenuous as gauze
And drifting loose like a white curtain
Vacillating in black night air
That holds white lilacs, God knows where.

"Close your eyes," said the inner ear;
"As night lookouts learn not to see
Ahead but only off one side,
As the eye's sight is never clear
But blind, dead center, you must be
Content; look not upon your bride
Till day's light lifts her eyelids wide."

I turned my back to her, set out
My own way back and let her follow
Like some curious albino beast
That prowls in areas of drought,
Lured past the town's slack doors, the hollow
Walls, the stream-bed lost in mist,
That breathless long climb, with no least

Doubt she must track me close behind;
As the actual scent of flesh, she must
Trail my voice unquestioning where.
Yet where the dawn first edged my mind
In one white flashing of mistrust
I turned and she, she was not there.
My hands closed on the high, thin air.

It was the nature of the thing:
No moon outlives its leaving night,
No sun its day. And I went on
Rich in the loss of all I sing
To the threshold of waking light,
To larksong and the live, gray dawn.
So night by night, my life has gone.

The Marsh

Swampstrife and spatterdock
　　lull in the heavy waters;
some thirty little frogs
　　spring with each step you walk;
a fish's belly glitters
　　tangled near rotting logs.

Over by the gray rocks
　　muskrats dip and circle.
Out of his rim of ooze
　　a silt-black pond snail walks
inverted on the surface
　　toward what food he may choose.

You look up; while you walk
　　the sun bobs and is snarled
in the enclosing weir
　　of trees, in their dead stalks.
Stick in the mud, old heart,
　　what are you doing here?

September in the Park

For Rita

This pinched face of the moon
   all afternoon
spies through the hanging smoke
that glows where maples, turning,
   recall for one
more hour the tarnished sun
in rust of their last burning.

Still, those who are out walking
   will hear the laughter
of drab, blue-chevroned ducks;
the drunkard echo mocking
   where they carouse
on minnow ponds still flowing.
Beyond the bare oak's
   reach of boughs,
as black as some charred rafter,
are slow and waiting flocks,
   but they are going.

This world is going
to leave the furnitures
of its unsheltering house
   in snow's dustcovers.
This old moon on its rounds
of the estate and grounds
   can well make sure
that no trespasser stirs
the fireplace or uncovers
   the burned out bed
of ashes. The young lovers
will not be coming here
   to give the bear

the offer of their bread.
This watchful face of age
   set pale and stern
over the gray iron cage
where his old habits turn
   and pace again
must mind his days to turn
him back in single, deep,
   cold-blooded sleep.

The hurrying, gray squirrels
   gather together
their hoard of the rich acorns
to their tall, windblown nest.
   And I, dear girl,
remember I have gathered
my hand upon your breast.

The Operation

From stainless steel basins of water
They brought warm cloths and they washed me,
From spun aluminum bowls, cold Zephiran sponges, fuming;
Gripped in the dead yellow glove, a bright straight razor
Inched on my stomach, down my groin,
Paring the brown hair off. They left me
White as a child, not frightened. I was not
Ashamed. They clothed me, then,
In the thin, loose, light, white garments,
The delicate sandals of poor Pierrot,
A schoolgirl first offering her sacrament.

I was drifting, inexorably, on toward sleep.
In skullcaps, masked, in blue-green gowns, attendants
Towed my cart, afloat in its white cloths,
The body with its tributary poisons borne
Down corridors of the diseased, thronging:
The scrofulous faces, contagious grim boys,
The huddled families, weeping, a staring woman
Arched to her gnarled stick,—a child was somewhere
Screaming, screaming—then, blind silence, the elevator rising
To the arena, humming, vast with lights; blank hero,
Shackled and spellbound, to enact my deed.

Into flowers, into women, I have awakened.
Too weak to think of strength, I have thought all day,
Or dozed among standing friends. I lie in night, now,
A small mound under linen like the drifted snow,
Only by nurses visited, in radiance, saying, Rest.
Opposite, ranked office windows glare; headlamps, below,
Trace out our highways; their cargoes under dark tarpaulins,
Trucks climb, thundering, and sirens may
Wail for the fugitive. It is very still. In my brandy bowl
Of sweet peas at the window, the crystal world
Is inverted, slow and gay.

Papageno

For Janice

Far in the woods my stealthy flute
Had jailed all gaudy feathered birds
And brought their songs back true to life;
Equipped with lime and quick salt, fruit
And fifty linking nets of words
I went to whistle up a wife.

My mouth was padlocked for a liar.
Losing what old hands never seek
To snare in their most cunning art,
I starved till my rib cage was wire
Under a towel. I could not speak
To hush this chattering, blue heart.

I beat about dead bushes where
No song starts and my cages stand
Bare in the crafty breath of you.
Night's lady, spreading your dark hair,
Come take this rare bird into hand;
In that deft cage, he might sing true.

Song

Sweet beast, I have gone prowling,
   a proud rejected man
who lived along the edges
   catch as catch can;
in darkness and in hedges
   I sang my sour tone
and all my love was howling
   conspicuously alone.

I curled and slept all day
   or nursed my bloodless wounds
until the squares were silent
   where I could make my tunes
singular and violent.
   Then, sure as hearers came
I crept and flinched away.
   And, girl, you've done the same.

A stray from my own type,
   led along by blindness,
my love was near to spoiled
   and curdled all my kindness.
I find no kin, no child;
   only the weasel's ilk.
Sweet beast, cat of my own stripe,
   come and take my milk.

Riddle

So small it is, there must be at least two
Helping each other see it. If each stands
Close enough he may come to be foureyed
And make their sight bifocal, looking through
Each other. If they act as a microscope
Of mounted powers it shall be magnified
Like an airy globe or beach ball that expands
Between them so vast they could never hope
To grasp it without all four of their hands
        Opened wide.

It lengthens, outstretched like a playing field
Where they stand as the two opposing goals
That can't be reached. Or it's a field of force,
Ethereal continuum, whereby they wield
Influence through matter, time and space
(Of all which it's the grave and radiant source),
Yet where attraction drives out their like souls
Across the expansive universe they've built as the poles
That only in circumference embrace
        And by divorce.

You have the damnedest friends and seem to think
You have some right to think. You have kept keen
Our arguments and souls so we have grown
Closely together where most people shrink.
You sleep tonight with threatening relations
In El Dorado; I am here alone
To tell you, *"Vive la difference!"* We have seen
The energetic first stuff of creation
So that today, if there's a world between
        Us, it's our own.

Song

Observe the cautious toadstools
   still on the lawn today
though they grow over-evening;
   sun shrinks them away.
Pale and proper and rootless,
   they righteously extort
their living from the living.
   I have been their sort.

See by our blocked foundation
   the cold, archaic clay,
stiff and clinging and sterile
   as children mold at play
or as the Lord God fashioned
   before He breathed it breath.
The earth we dig and carry
   for flowers, is strong in death.

Woman, we are the rich
   soil, friable and humble,
where all our murders rot,
   where our old deaths crumble
and fortify my reach
   far from you, wide and free,
though I have set my root
   in you and am your tree.

Seeing You Have . . .

Seeing you have a woman
Whose loves grow thick as the weeds
That keep songsparrows through the year,
Why are you envious of boys
Who prowl the streets all night in packs
So they are equal to the proud
Slender girls they fear?

She's like the tall grass, common,
That sends roots, where it needs,
Six feet into the prairies.
Why do you teach yourself the loud
Hankering voices of blue jays
That quarrel branch by branch to peck
And spoil the bitter cherries?

Home Town

I go out like a ghost,
nights, to walk the streets
I walked fifteen years younger—
seeking my old defeats,
devoured by the old hunger;
I had supposed

this longing and upheaval
had left me with my youth.
Fifteen years gone; once more,
the old lies are the truth:
I must prove I dare,
and the world, and love, is evil.

I have had loves, had such
honors as freely came;
it does not seem to matter.
Boys swagger just the same
along the curbs, or mutter
among themselves and watch.

They're out for the same prize.
And, as the evening grows,
the young girls take the street,
hard, in harlequin clothes,
with black shells on their feet
and challenge in their eyes.

Like a young bitch in her season
she walked the carnival
tonight, trailed by boys;
then, stopped at a penny stall
for me; by glittering toys
the pitchman called the reason

to come and take a chance,
try my hand, my skill.
I could not look; bereft
of breath, against my will,
I walked ahead and left
her there without one glance.

Pale soul, consumed by fear
of the living world you haunt,
have you learned what habits lead you
to hunt what you don't want;
learned who does not need you;
learned you are no one here?

A Cardinal

I wake late and leave
the refurbished quonset
where they let me live.
I feel like their leftovers:
they keep me for the onset
of some new war or other.

With half a ream of paper
and fountain pens, equipped
with ink and ink eraser,
a book to hunt up words,
and the same old manuscripts,
I tromp off to the woods,

the little stand of birches
between golf course and campus
where birds flirt through the branches
and the city will be hushed.
Inside this narrow compass
I crash through underbrush,

beer cans and lovers' trash
in search of my horizons
of meadowlark and thrush.
Yet near me, here, it's still.
I carry a scared silence
with me like my smell.

At each of my footsteps
one of the insect noises
in the tall grass, stops.
The weeds sing where I leave.
All the living voices
evade me like beliefs.

Well, let them look *me* up
and take their own sweet time;
I've come to set up shop
under this blue spruce
and tinker at my rhymes.
God knows it's little use;

God knows I have spent ages
peering like a stuffed owl
at these same blank pages
and, though I strained to listen,
the world lay wrapped with wool
far as the ends of distance.

And what do I hear today?
Little that sounds mine—
in town, across the way,
mill whistles squeal;
now, closer by, the whine
of a freight car's wheels;

out on the superturnpike
the cattle trucks and trailers
lumbering toward next week;
beyond, from the county airport,
where golf balls veer like tracers,
great engines thunder their part

in this devil's Mass
of marketable praise.
Oh, they've all found *their* voices.
And now I catch a meter
under this heavy prose
of factories and motors:

the college air cadets
are on their grinder, marching,
counting out their cadence,
one two three four, creating
for the school and market
the ground bass of our credo—

faith in free enterprise
and our unselfish forces
who chant to advertise
the ancient pulse of violence.
Meantime, I fuss with phrases
or clamp my jaws in silence.

Watch out; what's this red
bird, fluttering up to perch
ten feet from my head!
See the green insect wings,
pinched in his beak, twitch.
He swallows it. And sings.

Speak of the bloody devil!
Old sleek satanic cardinal—
you get your bellyful,
maintain the ancient Law,
and celebrate this ordinal
of the red beak and claw.

You natural Jesuit,
sing, in your fine feathers,
Hosannah to Appetite;
announce to the woods and hills
the one god of our fathers
is living in us still;

sing for the flyboys, birdy,
in praise of their profession;
sing for the choirs of pretty
slogans and catch-phrases
that rule us by obsession;
praise what it pays to praise:

praise soap and garbage cans,
join with the majority
in praising man-eat-man,
or praise the young who sell
their minds to retire at forty.
With honor.
                    Go to hell!

Good God! This is absurd!
A veritable scarecrow!
I curse out a poor bird
for daring feed his belly;
now my bird has flown
and left me in this gully.

It is absurd, absurd
Darwinian self-pity!
As if a self-made bird
would sign his days to sergeants,
his soul to a committee,
or call himself a bargain!

As if I'd never heard
what the birds' song means;
as if I'd ask a bird
to mortify his body.
Wait; from the next ravine,
he's singing again, already.

And he outspeaks a vital
claim to know his needs;
his song's a squatter's title
on his tree and the half acre
in which he hunts and breeds
and feeds the best he's able.

To enemies and rivals,
to mates and quick beetles,
he sings out for survival:
"I want my meals and loving;
I fight nobody's battles;
don't pardon me for living.

The world's not done to me;
it is what I do;
whom I speak shall be;
I music out my name
and what I tell is who
in all the world I am."

We whistle in the dark
of a region in doubt
where unknown powers work,
as watchmen in the night
ring bells to say, *Watch out,*
I am here; I have the right.

It should be recognized
I have not come sneaking
and look for no surprises.
Lives are saved this way.
Each trade has its way of speaking,
each bird its name to say.

We whistle in the dark
to drive the devils off.
Each dog creates his bark.
Even I, in Navy blues,
I whistled *Wachet Auf*
to tell the sailors who.

He's back; obliquely flying
under a trail of vapor,
our sky's white center-line.
A robin goes by, wrestling
a streamer of toiletpaper
his mate might want for nesting.

Selfish, unorthodox,
they live upon our leavings.
Boys or cats or hawks
can scare them out of song.
Still, long as they are living,
they are not still for long.

Each year the city leaves
less of trees or meadows;
they nest in our very eaves
and say what they have to say.
Assertion is their credo;
style tells their policy.

All bugs, now, and the birds
witness once more their voices
though I'm still in their weeds
tracking my specimen words,
replenishing the verses
of nobody else's world.

The Campus on the Hill

Up the reputable walks of old established trees
They stalk, children of the *nouveaux riches;* chimes
Of the tall Clock Tower drench their heads in blessing:
"I don't wanna play at your house;
I don't like you any more."
My house stands opposite, on the other hill,
Among meadows, with the orchard fences down and falling;
Deer come almost to the door.
You cannot see it, even in this clearest morning.
White birds hang in the air between
Over the garbage landfill and those homes thereto adjacent,
Hovering slowly, turning, settling down
Like the flakes sifting imperceptibly onto the little town
In a waterball of glass.
And yet, this morning, beyond this quiet scene,
The floating birds, the backyards of the poor,
Beyond the shopping plaza, the dead canal, the hillside
                              lying tilted in the air,

Tomorrow has broken out today:
Riot in Algeria, in Cyprus, in Alabama;
Aged in wrong, the empires are declining,
And China gathers, soundlessly, like evidence.
What shall I say to the young on such a morning?—
Mind is the one salvation?—also grammar?—
No; my little ones lean not toward revolt. They
Are the Whites, the vaguely furiously driven, who resist
Their souls with such passivity
As would make Quakers swear. All day, dear Lord, all day
They wear their godhead lightly.
They look out from their hill and say,
To themselves, "We have nowhere to go but down;
The great destination is to stay."
Surely the nations will be reasonable;
They look at the world—don't they?—the world's way?
The clock just now has nothing more to say.

27

April Inventory

The green catalpa tree has turned
All white; the cherry blooms once more.
In one whole year I haven't learned
A blessed thing they pay you for.
The blossoms snow down in my hair;
The trees and I will soon be bare.

The trees have more than I to spare.
The sleek, expensive girls I teach,
Younger and pinker every year,
Bloom gradually out of reach.
The pear tree lets its petals drop
Like dandruff on a tabletop.

The girls have grown so young by now
I have to nudge myself to stare.
This year they smile and mind me how
My teeth are falling with my hair.
In thirty years I may not get
Younger, shrewder, or out of debt.

The tenth time, just a year ago,
I made myself a little list
Of all the things I'd ought to know,
Then told my parents, analyst,
And everyone who's trusted me
I'd be substantial, presently.

I haven't read one book about
A book or memorized one plot.
Or found a mind I did not doubt.
I learned one date. And then forgot.
And one by one the solid scholars
Get the degrees, the jobs, the dollars.

And smile above their starchy collars.
I taught my classes Whitehead's notions;
One lovely girl, a song of Mahler's.
Lacking a source-book or promotions,
I showed one child the colors of
A luna moth and how to love.

I taught myself to name my name,
To bark back, loosen love and crying;
To ease my woman so she came,
To ease an old man who was dying.
I have not learned how often I
Can win, can love, but choose to die.

I have not learned there is a lie
Love shall be blonder, slimmer, younger;
That my equivocating eye
Loves only by my body's hunger;
That I have forces, true to feel,
Or that the lovely world is real.

While scholars speak authority
And wear their ulcers on their sleeves,
My eyes in spectacles shall see
These trees procure and spend their leaves.
There is a value underneath
The gold and silver in my teeth.

Though trees turn bare and girls turn wives,
We shall afford our costly seasons;
There is a gentleness survives
That will outspeak and has its reasons.
There is a loveliness exists,
Preserves us, not for specialists.

These Trees Stand . . .

These trees stand very tall under the heavens.
While *they* stand, if I walk, all stars traverse
This steep celestial gulf their branches chart.
Though lovers stand at sixes and at sevens
While civilizations come down with the curse,
Snodgrass is walking through the universe.

I can't make any world go around *your* house.
But note this moon. Recall how the night nurse
Goes ward-rounds, by the mild, reflective art
Of focusing her flashlight on her blouse.
Your name's safe conduct into love or verse;
Snodgrass is walking through the universe.

Your name's absurd, miraculous as sperm
And as decisive. If you can't coerce
One thing outside yourself, why you're the poet!
What irrefrangible atoms whirl, affirm
Their destiny and form Lucinda's skirts!
She can't make up your mind. Soon as you know it,
Your firmament grows touchable and firm.
If all this world runs battlefield or worse,
Come, let us wipe our glasses on our shirts:
Snodgrass is walking through the universe.

Heart's Needle

For Cynthia

When he would not return to fine
garments and good food, to his houses
and his people, Loingseachan told him,
"Your father is dead." "I'm sorry to
hear it," he said. "Your mother is
dead," said the lad. "All pity for me
has gone out of the world." "Your
sister, too, is dead." "The mild sun rests
on every ditch," he said; "a sister loves
even though not loved." "Suibhne, your
daughter is dead." "And an only
daughter is the needle of the heart."
"And Suibhne, your little boy, who
used to call you "Daddy"—he is dead."
"Aye," said Suibhne, "that's the drop
that brings a man to the ground."
He fell out of the yew tree;
Loingseachan closed his arms around
him and placed him in manacles.

—AFTER THE MIDDLE-IRISH ROMANCE,
THE MADNESS OF SUIBHNE

1

Child of my winter, born
When the new fallen soldiers froze
In Asia's steep ravines and fouled the snows,
When I was torn

By love I could not still,
By fear that silenced my cramped mind
To that cold war where, lost, I could not find
My peace in my will,

All those days we could keep
Your mind a landscape of new snow
Where the chilled tenant-farmer finds, below,
His fields asleep

In their smooth covering, white
As quilts to warm the resting bed
Of birth or pain, spotless as paper spread
For me to write,

And thinks: Here lies my land
Unmarked by agony, the lean foot
Of the weasel tracking, the thick trapper's boot;
And I have planned

My chances to restrain
The torments of demented summer or
Increase the deepening harvest here before
It snows again.

2
Late April and you are three; today
   We dug your garden in the yard.
  To curb the damage of your play,
Strange dogs at night and the moles tunneling,
   Four slender sticks of lath stand guard
     Uplifting their thin string.

So you were the first to tramp it down.
   And after the earth was sifted close
You brought your watering can to drown
All earth *and* us. But these mixed seeds are pressed
   With light loam in their steadfast rows.
      Child, we've done our best.

Someone will have to weed and spread
   The young sprouts. Sprinkle them in the hour
When shadow falls across their bed.
You should try to look at them every day
   Because when they come to full flower
      I will be away.

      3
The child between them on the street
Comes to a puddle, lifts his feet
   And hangs on their hands. They start
At the live weight and lurch together,
Recoil to swing him through the weather,
   Stiffen and pull apart.

We read of cold war soldiers that
Never gained ground, gave none, but sat
   Tight in their chill trenches.
Pain seeps up from some cavity
Through the ranked teeth in sympathy;
   The whole jaw grinds and clenches

Till something somewhere has to give.
It's better the poor soldiers live
In someone else's hands
Than drop where helpless powers fall
On crops and barns, on towns where all
Will burn. And no man stands.

For good, they sever and divide
Their won and lost land. On each side
Prisoners are returned
Excepting a few unknown names.
The peasant plods back and reclaims
His fields that strangers burned

And nobody seems very pleased.
It's best. Still, what must not be seized
Clenches the empty fist.
I tugged your hand, once, when I hated
Things less: a mere game dislocated
The radius of your wrist.

Love's wishbone, child, although I've gone
As men must and let you be drawn
Off to appease another,
It may help that a Chinese play
Or Solomon himself might say
I am your real mother.

4

No one can tell you why
the season will not wait;
the night I told you I
must leave, you wept a fearful rate
to stay up late.

Now that it's turning Fall,
we go to take our walk
among municipal
flowers, to steal one off its stalk,
to try and talk.

We huff like windy giants
scattering with our breath
gray-headed dandelions;
Spring is the cold wind's aftermath.
The poet saith.

But the asters, too, are gray,
ghost-gray. Last night's cold
is sending on their way
petunias and dwarf marigold,
hunched sick and old.

Like nerves caught in a graph,
the morning-glory vines
frost has erased by half
still scrawl across their rigid twines.
Like broken lines

of verses I can't make.
In its unraveling loom
we find a flower to take,
with some late buds that might still bloom,
back to your room.

Night comes and the stiff dew.
I'm told a friend's child cried
because a cricket, who
had minstreled every night outside
her window, died.

5

Winter again and it is snowing;
Although you are still three,
You are already growing
Strange to me.

You chatter about new playmates, sing
Strange songs; you do not know
Hey ding-a-ding-a-ding
Or where I go

Or when I sang for bedtime, *Fox
Went out on a chilly night,*
Before I went for walks
And did not write;

You never mind the squalls and storms
That are renewed long since;
Outside the thick snow swarms
Into my prints

And swirls out by warehouses, sealed,
Dark cowbarns, huddled, still,
Beyond to the blank field,
The fox's hill

Where he backtracks and sees the paw,
Gnawed off, he cannot feel;
Conceded to the jaw
Of toothed, blue steel.

6

Easter has come around
again; the river is rising
over the thawed ground
and the banksides. When you come you bring
an egg dyed lavender.
We shout along our bank to hear
our voices returning from the hills to meet us.
We need the landscape to repeat us.

You lived on this bank first.
While nine months filled your term, we knew
how your lungs, immersed
in the womb, miraculously grew
their useless folds till
the fierce, cold air rushed in to fill
them out like bushes thick with leaves. You took your hour,
caught breath, and cried with your full lung power.

Over the stagnant bight
we see the hungry bank swallow
    flaunting his free flight
still; we sink in mud to follow
    the killdeer from the grass
that hides her nest. That March there was
rain; the rivers rose; you could hear killdeers flying
    all night over the mudflats crying.

You bring back how the red-
winged blackbird shrieked, slapping frail wings,
    diving at my head—
I saw where her tough nest, cradled, swings
    in tall reeds that must sway
with the winds blowing every way.
If you recall much, you recall this place. You still
    live nearby—on the opposite hill.

After the sharp windstorm
of July Fourth, all that summer
    through the gentle, warm
afternoons, we heard great chain saws chirr
    like iron locusts. Crews
of roughneck boys swarmed to cut loose
branches wrenched in the shattering wind, to hack free
    all the torn limbs that could sap the tree.

In the debris lay
starlings, dead. Near the park's birdrun
    we surprised one day
a proud, tan-spatted, buff-brown pigeon.
    In my hands she flapped so
fearfully that I let her go.
Her keeper came. And we helped snarl her in a net.
    You bring things I'd as soon forget.

    You raise into my head
a Fall night that I came once more
    to sit on your bed;
sweat beads stood out on your arms and fore-
    head and you wheezed for breath,
for help, like some child caught beneath
its comfortable woolly blankets, drowning there.
    Your lungs caught and would not take the air.

    Of all things, only we
have power to choose that we should die;
    nothing else is free
in this world to refuse it. Yet I,
    who say this, could not raise
myself from bed how many days
to the thieving world. Child, I have another wife,
    another child. We try to choose our life.

7

Here in the scuffled dust
  is our ground of play.
I lift you on your swing and must
  shove you away,
see you return again,
  drive you off again, then

stand quiet till you come.
  You, though you climb
higher, farther from me, longer,
  will fall back to me stronger.
Bad penny, pendulum,
  you keep my constant time

to bob in blue July
  where fat goldfinches fly
over the glittering, fecund
  reach of our growing lands.
Once more now, this second,
  I hold' you in my hands.

8

I thumped on you the best I could
  which was no use;
you would not tolerate your food
until the sweet, fresh milk was soured
  with lemon juice.

That puffed you up like a fine yeast.
   The first June in your yard
like some squat Nero at a feast
you sat and chewed on white, sweet clover.
   That is over.

When you were old enough to walk
   we went to feed
the rabbits in the park milkweed;
saw the paired monkeys, under lock,
   consume each other's salt.

Going home we watched the slow
stars follow us down Heaven's vault.
You said, let's catch one that comes low,
   pull off its skin
   and cook it for our dinner.

   As absentee bread-winner,
I seldom got you such cuisine;
we ate in local restaurants
or bought what lunches we could pack
   in a brown sack

with stale, dry bread to toss for ducks
   on the green-scummed lagoons,
crackers for porcupine and fox,
life-savers for the footpad coons
   to scour and rinse,

snatch after in their muddy pail
   and stare into their paws.
When I moved next door to the jail
   I learned to fry
omelettes and griddlecakes so I

could set you supper at my table.
As I built back from helplessness,
   when I grew able,
the only possible answer was
   you had to come here less.

This Hallowe'en you come one week.
   You masquerade
   as a vermilion, sleek,
fat, crosseyed fox in the parade
or, where grim jackolanterns leer,

go with your bag from door to door
foraging for treats. How queer:
   when you take off your mask
my neighbors must forget and ask
   whose child you are.

Of course you lose your appetite,
   whine and won't touch your plate;
      as local law
I set your place on an orange crate
in your own room for days. At night

you lie asleep there on the bed
     and grate your jaw.
Assuredly your father's crimes
     are visited
on you. You visit me sometimes.

The time's up. Now our pumpkin sees
    me bringing your suitcase.
      He holds his grin;
the forehead shrivels, sinking in.
You break this year's first crust of snow

off the runningboard to eat.
    We manage, though for days
I crave sweets when you leave and know
they rot my teeth. Indeed our sweet
    foods leave us cavities.

9

    I get numb and go in
though the dry ground will not hold
    the few dry swirls of snow
and it must not be very cold.
A friend asks how you've been
    and I don't know

    or see much right to ask.
Or what use it could be to know.
    In three months since you came
the leaves have fallen and the snow;
your pictures pinned above my desk
    seem much the same.

Somehow I come to find
myself upstairs in the third floor
   museum's halls,
walking to kill my time once more
among the enduring and resigned
    stuffed animals,

   where, through a century's
caprice, displacement and
   known treachery between
its wars, they hear some old command
and in their peaceable kingdoms freeze
    to this still scene,

Nature Morte. Here
by the door, its guardian,
   the patchwork dodo stands
where you and your stepsister ran
laughing and pointing. Here, last year,
    you pulled my hands

and had your first, worst quarrel,
so toys were put up on your shelves.
   Here in the first glass cage
the little bobcats arch themselves,
still practicing their snarl
    of constant rage.

The bison, here, immense,
shoves at his calf, brow to brow,
    and looks it in the eye
to see what is it thinking now.
I forced you to obedience;
    I don't know why.

Still the lean lioness
beyond them, on her jutting ledge
    of shale and desert shrub,
stands watching always at the edge,
stands hard and tanned and envious
    above her cub;

with horns locked in tall heather,
two great Olympian Elk stand bound,
    fixed in their lasting hate
till hunger brings them both to ground.
Whom equal weakness binds together
    none shall separate.

Yet separate in the ocean
of broken ice, the white bear reels
    beyond the leathery groups
of scattered, drab Arctic seals
arrested here in violent motion
    like Napoleon's troops.

Our states have stood so long
at war, shaken with hate and dread,
    they are paralyzed at bay;
once we were out of reach, we said,
we would grow reasonable and strong.
        Some other day.

Like the cold men of Rome,
we have won costly fields to sow
    in salt, our only seed.
Nothing but injury will grow.
I write you only the bitter poems
        that you can't read.

Onan who would not breed
a child to take his brother's bread
    and be his brother's birth,
rose up and left his lawful bed,
went out and spilled his seed
        in the cold earth.

I stand by the unborn,
by putty-colored children curled
    in jars of alcohol,
that waken to no other world,
unchanging, where no eye shall mourn.
        I see the caul

that wrapped a kitten, dead.
I see the branching, doubled throat
    of a two-headed foal;
I see the hydrocephalic goat;
here is the curled and swollen head,
        there, the burst skull;

    skin of a limbless calf;
a horse's foetus, mummified;
    mounted and joined forever,
the Siamese twin dogs that ride
belly to belly, half and half,
        that none shall sever.

    I walk among the growths,
by gangrenous tissue, goiter, cysts,
    by fistulas and cancers,
where the malignancy man loathes
is held suspended and persists.
        And I don't know the answers.

    The window's turning white.
The world moves like a diseased heart
    packed with ice and snow.
Three months now we have been apart
less than a mile. I cannot fight
        or let you go.

10

The vicious winter finally yields
    the green winter wheat;
the farmer, tired in the tired fields
    he dare not leave, will eat.

Once more the runs come fresh; prevailing
    piglets, stout as jugs,
harry their old sow to the railing
    to ease her swollen dugs

and game colts trail the herded mares
    that circle the pasture courses;
our seasons bring us back once more
    like merry-go-round horses.

With crocus mouths, perennial hungers,
    into the park Spring comes;
we roast hot dogs on old coat hangers
    and feed the swan bread crumbs,

pay our respects to the peacocks, rabbits,
    and leathery Canada goose
who took, last Fall, our tame white habits
    and now will not turn loose.

In full regalia, the pheasant cocks
    march past their dubious hens;
the porcupine and the lean, red fox
    trot around bachelor pens

and the miniature painted train
   wails on its oval track:
you said, I'm going to Pennsylvania!
   and waved. And you've come back.

If I loved you, they said I'd leave
   and find my own affairs.
Well, once again this April, we've
   come around to the bears;

punished and cared for, behind bars,
   the coons on bread and water
stretch thin black fingers after ours.
   And you are still my daughter.

Remains

The Mother

She stands in the dead center like a star;
They form around her like her satellites
Taking her energies, her heat, light
And massive attraction on their paths, however far.

Born of her own flesh; still, she feels them drawn
Into the outer cold by dark forces;
They are in love with suffering and perversion,
With the community of pain. Thinking them gone,

Out of her reach, she is consoled by evil
In neighbors, children, the world she cannot change,
That lightless universe where they range
Out of the comforts of her disapproval.

If evil did not exist, she would create it
To die in righteousness, her martyrdom
To that sweet dominion they have bolted from.
Then, at last, she can think that she is hated

And is content. Things can decay, break,
Spoil themselves; who cares? She'll gather the debris
With loving tenderness to give them; she
Will weave a labyrinth of waste, wreckage

And hocus-pocus; leave free no fault
Or cornerhole outside those lines of force
Where she and only she can thread a course.
All else in her grasp grows clogged and halts.

Till one by one, the areas of her brain
Switch off and she has filled all empty spaces;
Now she hallucinates in their right places
Their after-images, reversed and faint.

And the drawn strands of love, spun in her mind,
Turn dark and cluttered, precariously hung
With the black shapes of her mates, her sapless young,
Where she moves by habit, hungering and blind.

Diplomacy: The Father

Your mission, in any disputed area, is to find
    (as in yourself)
which group, which element among the contending forces
    seems, by nature, most fit to take control.
Stronger perhaps, more driven, gifted with resources—
    no matter: able to bind in a firm goal
the ennervating local passions native to our kind.
      That force, of course, is

your enemy—whom you cannot choose but love.
      As in yourself,
it's this, it's those so loved, that can grow oppressive
    and steal your hard-bought freedom to choose
that you won't love. Act loving, then. Make no aggressive
    move; make friends. Make, though, for future use,
notes on their debts, beliefs, whom they're most fond of—
      their weaknesses. If

anything, appear more loyal—pretend to feel
      as in yourself
you'd truly want to feel: affectionate and admiring.
    Then hate grows, discovering the way such foes enslave
you worst: if you loved them, you'd *feel* free. Conspiring
    to outwit such subtlety, devise and save
good reasons for your hatred; count wounds. Conceal,
      though, this entire ring

of proofs, excuses, wrongs which you maintain
      as in yourself
might harbor some benign, enfeebling growth.
    As for followers, seek those who'll take your aid:
the weak. In doubt who's weaker, finance both.
    Collect the dawdlers, the brilliant but afraid,
the purchasable losers—those who, merely to gain
      some power they can loathe,

would quite as willingly be out of power
      as in. Yourself?—
friend, this is lonely work. Deep cravings will persist
    for true allies, for those you love; you will long
to speak your mind out sometimes, or to assist
    someone who, given that help, might grow strong
and admirable. You've reached your bleakest hour,
      the pitiless test.

But think: why let your own aid diminish you?
      As in yourself,
so in those who take your help, your values or your name,
    you've sought out their best thoughts, their hidden talents
only to buy out, to buy off. Your fixed aim,
    whatever it costs, must still be for a balance
of power in the family, the firm, the whole world through.
      Exactly the same

as a balance of impotence—in any group or nation
      as in yourself.
Suppose some one of them rose up and could succeed
    your foe—he'd *be* your foe. To underlings, dispense
all they can ask, but don't need; give till they need
    your giving. One gift could free them: confidence.
They'd never dare ask. Betray no dedication
      to any creed

or person—talk high ideals; then you'll be known
      as, in yourself,
harmless. Exact no faith from them, no affection;
    suppose they've learned no loyalty to you—
that's one step taken in the right direction.
    Never forbid them. Let no one pay back what's due;
the mere air they breathe should come as a loan
      beyond collection.

Like air, you must be everywhere at once, where-
        as, in your self-
defense, make yourself scarce. Your best disguise
    is to turn gray, spreading yourself so thin
you're one with all unknowns—essential. Vaporize
    into the fog all things that happen, happen in
or fail to happen. In the end, you have to appear
        as unworldly in the eyes

of this whole sanctioned world that your care drained
        as in yours. Self-
sacrifice has borne you, then, through that destruction
    programmed into life; you live on in that loving tension
you leave to those who'll still take your instruction.
    You've built their world; an air of soft suspension
which you survive in, as cradled and sustained
        as in yourself.

The Mouse

I remember one evening—we were small—
Playing outdoors, we found a mouse,
A dusty little gray one, lying
By the side steps. Afraid he might be dead,
We carried him all around the house
On a piece of tinfoil, crying.

Ridiculous children; we could bawl
Our eyes out about nothing. Still,
How much violence had we seen?
They teach you—quick—you have to be well-bred
In all events. We can't all win.
Don't whine to get your will.

We live with some things, after all,
Bitterer than dying, cold as hate:
The old insatiable loves,
That vague desire that keeps watch overhead,
Polite, wakeful as a cat,
To tease us with our lives;

That pats at you, wants to see you crawl
Some, then picks you back alive;
That needs you just a little hurt.
The mind goes blank, then the eyes. Weak with dread,
In shock, the breath comes short;
We go about our lives.

And then the little animal
Plays out; the dulled heart year by year
Turns from its own needs, forgets its grief.
Asthmatic, timid, twenty-five, unwed—
The day we left you by your grave,
I wouldn't spare one tear.

Viewing the Body

Flowers like a gangster's funeral;
  Eyeshadow like a whore.
They all say isn't she beautiful.
  She, who never wore

Lipstick or such a dress,
  Never got taken out,
Was scarcely looked at, much less
  Wanted or talked about;

Who, gray as a mouse, crept
  The dark halls at her mother's
Or snuggled, soft, and slept
  Alone in the dim bedcovers.

Today at last she holds
  All eyes and a place of honor
Till the obscene red folds
  Of satin close down on her.

Disposal

The unworn long gown, meant for dances
She would have scarcely dared attend,
Is fobbed off on a friend—
Who can't help wondering if it's spoiled
But thinks, well, she can take her chances.

We roll her spoons up like old plans
Or failed securities, seal their case,
Then lay them back. One lace
Nightthing lies in the chest, unsoiled
By wear, untouched by human hands.

We don't dare burn those canceled patterns
And markdowns that she actually wore,
Yet who do we know so poor
They'd take them? Spared all need, all passion,
Saved from loss, she lies boxed in satins

Like a pair of party shoes
That seemed to never find a taker;
We send back to its maker
A life somehow gone out of fashion
But still too good to use.

Fourth of July

The drifting smoke is gone, today,
From the mill chimneys; the laborers from the great
Iron foundries are on strike. They celebrate
Their Independence her own way.

She stopped a year ago today.
Firecrackers mark the occasion down the street;
I thumb through magazines and keep my seat.
What can anybody say?

In her room, nights, we lie awake
By racks of unworn party dresses, shoes,
Her bedside asthma pipe, the glasses whose
Correction no one else will take.

Stuffed dogs look at us from the shelf
When we sit down together at the table.
You put a face on things the best you're able
And keep your comments to yourself.

It is a hideous mistake.
My young wife, unforgivably alive,
Takes a deep breath and blows out twenty-five
Candles on her birthday cake.

It is agreed she'll get her wish.
The candles smell; smoke settles through the room
Like a cheap stage set for Juliet's tomb.
I leave my meal cold on the dish.

We take the children to the park
To watch the fireworks and the marching band.
For hours a drill team pivots at command.
For hours we sit in the dark

Hearing some politician fume;
Someone leads out a blonde schoolgirl to crown
Queen of this war-contract factory town;
Skyrockets and the last guns boom.

I keep my seat and wonder where,
Into what ingrown nation has she gone
Among a people silent and withdrawn;
I wonder in the stifling air

Of what deprived and smoke-filled town
They brush together and do not feel lust,
Hope, rage, love; within what senseless dust
Is she at home to settle down;

Where do they know her, and the dead
Meet in a vacancy of shared disgrace,
Keep an old holiday of blame and place
Their tinsel wreathe on her dark head?

We tramp home through the sulfurous smoke
That is my father's world. Now we must
Enter my mother's house of lint and dust
She could not breathe; I wheeze and choke.

It is an evil, stupid joke:
My wife is pregnant; my sister's in her grave.
We live in the home of the free and of the brave.
No one would hear me, even if I spoke.

The Survivors

We wondered what might change
Once you were not here;
Tried to guess how they would rearrange
Their life, now you were dead. Oh, it was strange
Coming back this year—

To find the lawn unkept
And the rock gardens dense
With bindweed; the tangling rosebushes crept
And squandered over everything except
The trash by the fence;

The rose trellises blown
Down and still sprawled there;
Broken odd ends of porch furniture thrown
Around the yard; everything overgrown
Or down in disrepair.

On the tree they still protect
From the ungoverned gang
Of neighbor boys—eaten with worms, bird-pecked,
But otherwise uncared-for and unpicked,
The bitter cherries hang,

Brown and soft and botched.
The ground is thick with flies.
Around in front, two white stone lions are crouched
By the front steps; someone has patched
Cement across their eyes.

The Venetian blinds are drawn;
Inside, it is dark and still.
Always upon some errand, one by one,
They go from room to room, vaguely, in the wan
Half-light, deprived of will.

Mostly they hunt for some-
thing they've misplaced; otherwise
They turn the pages of magazines and hum
Tunelessly. At any time they come
To pass, they drop their eyes.

Only at night they meet.
By voiceless summoning
They come to the living room; each repeats
Some words he has memorized; each takes his seat
In the hushed, expectant ring

By the television set.
No one can draw his eyes
From that unnatural, cold light. They wait.
The screen goes dim and they hunch closer yet,
As the image dies.

In the cellar where the sewers
Rise, unseen, the pale white
Ants grow in decaying stacks of old newspapers.
Outside, street lamps appear, and friends of yours
Call children in for the night.

And you have been dead one year.
Nothing is different here.

To a Child

We've taken the dog out for his walk
    To the practice football field;
We sit on a dead branch, concealed
In the scraggly brush and trees
Beside the stale, old spring; we talk our talk
    About the birds and the bees.

How strange we should come here.
In the thick, matted grass, ten feet away,
    Some twenty years ago I lay
      With my first girl. Half-dead
Or half-demented with my fear,
    I left her there and fled.

Still, I guess we often choose
Odd spots: we used to go stone-dapping
On the riverbanks where lovers lay
Abandoned in each others' arms all day
    By their beached, green canoes;
    You asked why were they napping.

We've sat on cemetery
Stones to sing; found a toad
Run over on the graveyard road
That no one had seen fit to bury;
    We've deciphered dark
Names carved in stone, names in the white birch bark.

We've waded up the creek
Over sharp stones and through deep
Slime, toward its source; caught a turtle
And carried the thing home to keep.
    At best, he lived a week.
We said that ought to make the garden fertile.

We learned the animal orders' name-
    tags, posted in the park;
We fed the llamas, fawns and goats that roam
    The childrens' zoo, a sort of Ark
    For the newborn, hurt or tame,
      A home away from home.

We heard a bantie chick there that had wandered
    Into the wrong pen
    Peeping, peeping, scurrying
    After a huge indignant hen
      That fled. You said we'd bring
    Our feather duster to crawl under.

    And I mailed you long letters
    Though you were still too young to read;
    I sent you maple wings that fly,
Linden gliders and torqued ailanthus seeds,
    Pine cones crammed with flyers that flutter
      Like soft moths down the sky;

    Told you how Fall winds bear
    The tree seeds out, like airmailed letters,
To a distant ground so, when they come up later,
    They will find, possibly,
    Rain, sun and the soil they need
      Far from the parent tree.

    They threw my letters out.
    Said I had probably forgotten.
    Well, we have seen the glow of rotten
Wood, the glimmering being that consumes
    The flesh of a dead trout.
    We have walked through living rooms

And seen the way the dodder,
That pale white parasitic love-vine, thrives
    Coiling the zinnias in the ardor
        Of its close embrace.
    We have watched grown men debase
    Themselves for their embittered wives

    And we have seen an old sow that could smother
        The sucklings in her stye,
    That could devour her own farrow.
We have seen my sister in her narrow
    Casket. Without love we die;
        With love we kill each other.

    You are afraid, now, of dying;
        Sick with change and loss;
    You think of your own self lying
Still in the ground while someone takes your room.
    Today, you felt the small life toss
        In your stepmother's womb.

    I sit here by you in the summer's lull
Near the lost handkerchiefs of lovers
        To tell you when your brother
    Will be born; how, and why.
    I tell you love is possible.
        We have to try.

The Boy
Made of Meat
A Poem for Children

Why do they make boys out of meat?
Whenever I sit down to eat
They say, "Sit up. Don't swing your feet.
You'll spill that milk. Now have some meat."

I say, "I've heard cupcakes taste good
With marmalade; I'll bet they would."
They say, "You know that's much too sweet
For growing boys. Here; take some meat."

I say, "Or some cream puffs with these
Dill pickles—would you pass that, please?"
They say, "Just sit down in that seat
And drop those cookies. Eat that meat!"

I say, "Ice cream with nuts would do;
But no candy—not till I'm through."
They jump up; they all stamp their feet:
"No! NO!! You need your meat, Meat, MEAT!!!"

"Sweet stuff makes you grow weak and fat—
You're not built out of things like that.
A growing boy's made out of meat;
Meat's the one thing all boys must eat."

What makes them think I can't grow strong
Except with meat? They must be wrong:
Why, right now I feel weak and sick
To see my plate get piled up thick

With meat, Meat, MEAT. I'd tell them so;
They'd say, "Get straight to bed, then," though;
"Bed's where all sick boys belong."
All the same, though, I know they're wrong.

71

A growing cow finds all he needs
To get strong eating grass and weeds.
I'll say, "Please help yourself and pass
The weeds. Here; have some nice, fresh grass."

Horses don't eat their meat at all;
They grow up strong and fast and tall.
Sometime try feeding meat to one—
You'll see how fast horses can run!

Just take one look at elephants:
They never eat *their* meat—not once.
If I ate peanuts till I got
That big, I'd show them what was what!

Why, they've been mixed up, all along;
Meat isn't how to grow up strong.
Just think of all the ones that do
Eat meat—think what they grow into:

Frogs eat their bugs up—each last bit;
They don't get big or strong from it.
Cats eat their mice—raw mice at that!
I'm bigger *now* than any cat.

And what if boys *are* made of meat:
We don't turn into what we eat—
It turns to us! Each cow I've seen
Ate grass; not one of them was green.

Our cat eats birds—she's got no wings;
Those birds don't help her when she sings!
Mice don't look like cheese and what's
More, squirrels don't look much like nuts.

Then, what if they were right? If we
Ate beefsteak just think what we'd be!
Next time they say, "Beef's good for you,"
I'll swish my tail up and say, "Moo!"

They say, "Eat meat so you'll grow big."
I'll say, "I thought you said, 'Don't be a pig!' "
Or when we've got pork for a meal
I'll just roll in the mud and squeal.

The way they pile meat on my dish,
Why, I could grow scales like a fish,
Horns like a sheep, feet like a hen—
I guess they'd all feel sorry then!

Still, here's what they should feel afraid of:
If we should eat just what we're made of
And growing boys are made of meat—
People are what we'd ought to eat!

Maybe they're right; maybe I'm wrong;
I'll eat my meat and grow up strong
Like good lions or good tigers do—
They won't keep *me* locked in some zoo:

I'd prowl down the main street of town
To see if any meat's around;
All the folks I'd meet I'd say,
"My, but you *do* look good today!"

Wouldn't they pat me on the head
And rub my ears while they all said,
"Good boy! You're so big and well-fed;
That's enough meat—try cake instead."

I'd sniff them over; then I'd roar,
"No sweet stuff! Meat! I want more! MORE!!
Just meat, Meat, MEAT!!! A man-sized steak!
I need some for this stomach-ache!"

I'd eat my meat up till I grew
So big that they'd see who was who;
They'd never say, "Please just get finished";
They'd say, "I like you small and thinnish;

"Why not just dawdle?" since they knew
They'd all be gone if I got through.
I'd eat it all up 'till I'd grown
So whopping, I'd be left alone.

Alone?—just wait now. That could be
Some trouble. Who'd look after me?
Where would I go, then, to get food?
Who'd fix it for me?—no one would!

And who'd fuss at me to get done?
Eating *that* much meat's no darn fun!
I may let meat folks stick around
Just till some better setup's found—

Till the great Topsy Turvy comes
And his voice booms like ten bass drums:
"Let everything around here change;
Let everything be good and strange.

"Kittens will chase big dogs up trees;
Flowers will chase the bumblebees;
Foxes will run from hens and hide;
Rocks will catch cold and come inside;

"Mothers will just love lots of noise;
Fathers will smile at naughty boys;
Grandparents will act strict and mean;
Nothing will be the way it's been.

"And boys? We'll make boys from mince pies—
That ought to grow boys the right size;
We'll make boys out of gum and candy—
That ought to build boys brisk and dandy;

"We'll make boys out of plum preserves
To build strong muscles and quick nerves;
We'll make boys out of cakes and tarts
To give them rich blood and stout hearts;

"Make them from popcorn, pecans, pickles,
Jam, jelly, crackerjack, Popsicles,
Ice cream with toppings sweet and sour;
We'll make those boys just bulge with power!"

Then, then, when I sit down to eat
They'll say, "Slide down in your seat;
Don't sit so tall! Please swing your feet.
And don't just sit there looking sweet!

You finish all that candy! Stop;
Don't eat that meat! Now drink your pop!"

After Experience

Partial Eclipse

*Last night's eclipse, 99 percent
complete, seemed at times to be
total because of light mists
and low-hanging clouds.*

—RADIO NEWS REPORT

Once we'd packed up your clothes
    It was something to talk about:
The full moon, how it rose
    Red, went pale, then went out

As that slow shadow crossed—
    The way Time might erase
Its blackboard: one cheek lost,
    The eyes, most of the face

Hovering dim as a ghost,
    Or the dark print of some light
That seared the eyes, almost,
    Yet lives in the lids, clenched tight.

But still one brilliant sliver
    Stayed, worrying the eye,
Till even that would shiver,
    Go sick and the whole sky—

We wished it all blank, bereft.
    But no; the mists drifted on;
Something, one glint was left.
    Next morning you had gone.

September

In town, your friends play hide-and-seek
   In dead leaves piled by the sidewalk.
Today I hiked along the creek,
   Through dry weeds and the sharp oat stalks,

Carrying my old binoculars;
   I hoped to spot that small Green Heron
We saw together down the marsh
   This August. He'd gone off on an errand.

Then too, of course, this *is* September.
   The newts in the creek had gone, already.
I don't know where. I can't remember
   Your face or anything you said.

Reconstructions

This fall, we left your Grandma's
And had to leave your plant behind;
You said if no one watered it
And it would die, you didn't mind.
You mean to play the zinnia
In some sorry melodrama.

You offered me, one day, your doll
To sing songs to, bubble and nurse,
And said that was her birthday;
You reappeared then, grabbed her away,
Said just don't mess with her at all;
It was your child, yours.

And earlier this summer, how
You would tell the dog he had to "Stay!"
Then always let him sit
There, ears up, tense, all
Shivering to hear you call;
You turned and walked away.

We are like patients who rehearse
Old unbearable scenes
Day after day after day.
I memorize you, bit by bit,
And must restore you in my verses
To sell to magazines.

We keep what our times allow
And turn our grief into play.
We left you at your mother's; now
We've given the dog away.

The First Leaf

The first leaf, as we drive off,
Spins down the windshield, red;
Birds flock near the driveway.
We say what has to be said:

Autumn, winter, spring,
We'll write our usual letter;
One month for each finger.
And this makes you feel better.

We park by a transport trailer
Of bawling, white-faced cattle
That stare between the truck rails
Like men being shipped to battle,

Perhaps, in some other country,
But who will ever know?
From somewhere down the station
I hear a rooster crow.

Next year we'll hardly know you;
Still, all the blame endures.
This year you will live at our expense;
We have a life at yours,

Now I can earn a living
By turning out elegant strophes.
Your six-year teeth lie on my desk
Like a soldier's trophies.

You move off where I send you;
The train pulls down its track.
We go about our business;
I have turned my back.

Mementos, 1

Sorting out letters and piles of my old
   Canceled checks, old clippings, and yellow note cards
That meant something once, I happened to find
   Your picture. *That* picture. I stopped there cold,
Like a man raking piles of dead leaves in his yard
      Who has turned up a severed hand.

Still, that first second, I was glad: you stand
   Just as you stood—shy, delicate, slender,
In that long gown of green lace netting and daisies
   That you wore to our first dance. The sight of you stunned
Us all. Well, our needs were different, then,
      And our ideals came easy.

Then through the war and those two long years
   Overseas, the Japanese dead in their shacks
Among dishes, dolls, and lost shoes; I carried
   This glimpse of you, there, to choke down my fear,
Prove it had been, that it might come back.
      That was before we got married.

—Before we drained out one another's force
   With lies, self-denial, unspoken regret
And the sick eyes that blame; before the divorce
   And the treachery. Say it: before we met. Still,
I put back your picture. Someday, in due course,
      I will find that it's still there.

What We Said

Stunned in that first estrangement,
We went through the turning woods
Where inflamed leaves sick as words
Spun, wondering what the change meant.

Half gone, our road led onwards
By barbed wire, past the ravine
Where a lost couch, snarled in vines,
Spilled its soiled, gray innards

Into a garbage mound.
We came, then, to a yard
Where tarpaper, bottles and charred
Boards lay on the trampled ground.

This had been someone's lawn.
And, closing up like a wound,
The cluttered hole in the ground
A life had been built upon.

In the high grass, cars had been.
On the leafless branches, rags
And condoms fluttered like the flags
Of new orders moving in.

We talked of the last war, when
Houses, cathedral towns, shacks—
Whole continents went into wreckage.
What fools could do that again?

Ruin on every side—
We would set our loves in order,
Surely, we told each other.
Surely. That's what we said.

Lying Awake

This moth caught in the room tonight
Squirmed up, sniper-style, between
The rusty edges of the screen;
Then, long as the room stayed light,

Lay here, content, in some cornerhole.
Now that we've settled into bed
Though, he can't sleep. Overhead,
He hurls himself at the blank wall.

Each night hordes of these flutterers haunt
And climb my study windowpane;
Fired by reflection, their insane
Eyes gleam; they know what they want.

How do the petulant things survive?
Out in the fields they have a place
And proper work, furthering the race;
Why this blind fanatical drive

Indoors? Why rush at every spark,
Cigar, headlamp or railway warning
To knock off your wings and starve by morning?
And what could a moth fear in the dark

Compared with what you meet inside?
Still, he rams the fluorescent face
Of the clock, thinks that's another place
Of light and families, where he'll hide.

We'd ought to trap him in a jar,
Or come, like the white-coats, with a net
And turn him out toward living. Yet
We don't; we take things as they are.

Lobsters in the Window

First, you think they are dead.
Then you are almost sure
One is beginning to stir.
Out of the crushed ice, slow
As the hands of a schoolroom clock,
He lifts his one great claw
And holds it over his head;
Now, he is trying to walk.

But like a run-down toy;
Like the backward crabs we boys
Splashed after in the creek,
Trapped in jars or a net,
And then took home to keep.
Overgrown, retarded, weak,
He is fumbling yet
From the deep chill of his sleep

As if, in a glacial thaw,
Some ancient thing might wake
Sore and cold and stiff
Struggling to raise one claw
Like a defiant fist;
Yet wavering, as if
Starting to swell and ache
With that thick peg in the wrist.

I should wave back, I guess.
But still in his permanent clench
He's fallen back with the mass
Heaped in their common trench
Who stir, but do not look out
Through the rainstreaming glass,
Hear what the newsboys shout,
Or see the raincoats pass.

Looking

What was I looking for today?
All that poking under the rugs,
Peering under the lamps and chairs,
Or going from room to room that way,
Forever up and down the stairs
Like someone stupid with sleep or drugs.

Everywhere I was, was wrong.
I started turning the drawers out, then
I was staring in at the icebox door
Wondering if I'd been there long
Wondering what I was looking for.
Later on, I think I went back again.

Where did the rest of the time go?
Was I down cellar? I can't recall
Finding the light switch, or the last
Place I've had it, or how I'd know
I didn't look at it and go past.
Or whether it's what I want, at all.

A Friend

I walk into your house, a friend.
Your kids swarm up my steep hillsides
Or swing in my branches. Your boy rides
Me for his horsie; we pretend
Some troll threatens our lady fair.
I swing him squealing through the air
And down. Just what could I defend?

I tuck them in, sometimes, at night.
That's one secret we never tell.
Giggling in their dark room, they yell
They love me. Their father, home tonight,
Sees your girl curled up on my knee
And tells her "git"—she's bothering me.
I nod; she'd better think he's right.

Once they're in bed, he calls you "dear."
The boob-tube shows some hokum on
Adultery and loss; we yawn
Over a stale joke book and beer
Till it's your bedtime. I must leave.
I watch that squat toad pluck your sleeve.
As always, you stand shining near

Your window. I stand, Prince of Lies
Who's seen bliss; now I can drive back
Home past wreck and car lot, past shack
Slum and steelmill reddening the skies,
Past drive-ins, the hot pits where our teens
Fingerfuck and that huge screen's
Images fill their vacant eyes.

Leaving the Motel

Outside, the last kids holler
Near the pool: they'll stay the night.
Pick up the towels; fold your collar
Out of sight.

Check: is the second bed
Unrumpled, as agreed?
Landlords have to think ahead
In case of need,

Too. Keep things straight: don't take
The matches, the wrong keyrings—
We've nowhere we could keep a keepsake—
Ashtrays, combs, things

That sooner or later others
Would accidentally find.
Check: take nothing of one another's
And leave behind

Your license number only,
Which they won't care to trace;
We've paid. Still, should such things get lonely,
Leave in their vase

An aspirin to preserve
Our lilacs, the wayside flowers
We've gathered and must leave to serve
A few more hours;

That's all. We can't tell when
We'll come back, can't press claims;
We would no doubt have other rooms then,
Or other names.

The Lovers Go Fly a Kite

What's up, today, with our lovers?
  Only bright tatters—a kite
That plunges and bobs where it hovers
  At no improbable height.

It's shuddery like a hooked fish
  Or a stallion. They reel in string
And sprint, compassing their wish:
  To keep in touch with the thing.

They tear up their shirts for a tail
  In hopes that might steady
It down. Wobbling, frail,
  They think it may now be ready

And balance their hawk aloft—
  Poor moth of twigs and tissue
That would spill if one chill wind coughed,
  Dive down to tear, or to kiss you;

Yet still tugs the line they keep
  Like some exquisite sting ray
Hauled from a poisonous deep
  To explore the bright coasts of day,

Or say it's their weather ear
  Keeping the heart's patrol of
A treacherous, washed-out year,
  Searching for one sprig of olive.

What air they breathe is wrung
  With twenty subtleties;
Sharp bones of failure, hung
  In all the parkway trees;

It's enough to make you laugh—
  In these uncommitted regions
On an invisible staff
  To run up an allegiance!

Regraduating the Lute

Having gathered power and resonance
   Through two years' playing, the finger board
Replaned to the warp of the living grain, then
   We are ready. Keeping the strings
Tuned and under tension, we gradually
   Pare away, while playing constantly,
All excess from behind the tempered face.
   The way a long grief hollows the cheeks away.
Not so much as might lose
   Endurance to sustain a music,
Yet until the sounding board is parchment-
   thin, and the white bonestructure or a strong
Light would shine nearly through.
   Until it trembles to the least touch,
Trembles to the lightest song.
   By hand we slowly rub away
The preserving brilliant varnish to a soft
   Old silver glow. Its voice now
Is equal to any in the world. We take it
   Home to sing to or lay it on the bed.
In any place, at any time I play,
   Behind this face where nobody can see
I have burned your name. To stay.

The Examination

Under the thick beams of that swirly smoking light,
    The black robes are clustering, huddled in together.
Hunching their shoulders, they spread short, broad sleeves like night-
    Black grackles' wings; then they reach bone-yellow leather-

y fingers, each to each. And are prepared. Each turns
    His single eye—or since one can't discern their eyes,
That reflective, single, moon-pale disc which burns
    Over each brow—to watch this uncouth shape that lies

Strapped to their table. One probes with his ragged nails
    The slate-sharp calf, explores the thigh and the lean thews
Of the groin. Others raise, red as piratic sails,
    His wing, stretching, trying the pectoral sinews.

One runs his finger down the whet of that cruel
    Golden beak, lifts back the horny lids from the eyes,
Peers down in one bright eye malign as a jewel,
    And steps back suddenly. "He is anaesthetized?"

"He is. He is. Yes. Yes." The tallest of them, bent
    Down by the head, rises: "This drug possesses powers
Sufficient to still all gods in this firmament.
    This is Garuda who was fierce. He's yours for hours.

"We shall continue, please." Now, once again, he bends
    To the skull, and its clamped tissues. Into the cran-
ial cavity, he plunges both of his hands
    Like obstetric forceps and lifts out the great brain,

Holds it aloft, then gives it to the next who stands
	Beside him. Each, in turn, accepts it, although loath,
Turns it this way, that way, feels it between his hands
	Like a wasp's nest or some sickening outsized growth.

They must decide what thoughts each part of it must think;
	They tap at, then listen beside, each suspect lobe;
Next, with a crow's quill dipped into India ink,
	Mark on its surface, as if on a map or globe,

Those dangerous areas which need to be excised.
	They rinse it, then apply antiseptics to it;
Now silver saws appear which, inch by inch, slice
	Through its ancient folds and ridges, like thick suet.

It's rinsed, dried, and daubed with thick salves. The smoky saws
	Are scrubbed, resterilized, and polished till they gleam.
The brain is repacked in its case. Pinched in their claws,
	Glimmering needles stitch it up, that leave no seam.

Meantime, one of them has set blinders to the eyes,
	Inserted light packing beneath each of the ears
And caulked the nostrils in. One, with thin twine, ties
	The genitals off. With long wooden-handled shears,

Another chops pinions out of the scarlet wings.
	It's hoped that with disuse he will forget the sky
Or, at least, in time, learn, among other things,
	To fly no higher than his superiors fly.

Well; that's a beginning. The next time, they can split
    His tongue and teach him to talk correctly, can give
Him opinions on fine books and choose clothing fit
    For the integrated area where he'll live.

Their candidate may live to give them thanks one day.
    He will recover and may hope for such success
He might return to join their ranks. Bowing away,
    They nod, whispering, "One of ours; one of ours. Yes. Yes."

Flash Flood

The worst is over; the people
are all glad
to show you where it passed, scattering
paving bricks like handbills, elbowed
STOP
signs into respectful
attitudes, then filched the smug
porch off a house.
They lead you to a black hole where
it broke straight
through one block wall of a basement, then
as if appalled by something found in there,
broke back out through the opposite wall.
They will recite
the history of its progress:
its small beginnings in the hills; down
what gulleys it had gathered mud and power,
gathered rock, stumps, dead trees; gathering body
parts and boulders, engines, armchairs, train wheels, gathering
down into the town.
They argue over who first
spotted it, bubbling out of sewers;
recognized its stench; who heard it, angering
back of the welding shops and car barns; argue, finally,
where had it clambered over the creek banks, rioting
down their stunned streets, irresistibly splintering
the goods they had used their
lives collecting. For years
of skimping, hard work,
jockeying for position; for all
their small, reluctant, timorous swindlings;
for their dedication—this
is their reward. They talk about it
with such pride, you'd think
it was their own.
Think back how the orderlies danced while

bombs crazed their bunker
and the Third Reich died.
Think of the Thirties—of all those
who saw their lives totter and
falter and
go under, finally;
then began to live. Who
would not like to kick
some pretty girl?
The firemen clump around in their boots, now,
on one of the porches, talking
to the young Italian, loud, who owns it,
whom everybody watches;
he has achieved, at last, celebrity of a kind—
his kitchen departed like an excursion steamer;
he clutches his shirtfront like some short-legged Oedipus
and seems, for once, one with his destiny.
Meantime, his neighbors who have not, these many months,
found time to address each other
saunter about with coffee and extra bedding;
surprised as refugees, they may
shake hands; or will walk together, like prisoners
out for exercise. They watch
three tow trucks strain to resurrect the bones
of next year's Chevrolet, junked in the creek.
Isn't it terrible, they ask. Their eyes
are glittering with the flares and searchlights.
Awful, they say. And they may stay up, now,
probably, talking, half the night.

"After Experience Taught Me . . ."

After experience taught me that all the ordinary
Surroundings of social life are futile and vain;

> I'm going to show you something very
> Ugly: someday, it might save your life.

Seeing that none of the things I feared contain
In themselves anything either good or bad

> What if you get caught without a knife;
> Nothing—even a loop of piano wire;

Excepting only in the effect they had
Upon my mind, I resolved to inquire

> Take the first two fingers of this hand;
> Fork them out—kind of a "V for Victory"—

Whether there might be something whose discovery
Would grant me supreme, unending happiness.

> And jam them into the eyes of your enemy.
> You have to do this hard. Very hard. Then press

No virtue can be thought to have priority
Over this endeavor to preserve one's being.

> Both fingers down around the cheekbone
> And setting your foot high into the chest

No man can desire to act rightly, to be blessed,
To live rightly, without simultaneously

> You must call up every strength you own
> And you can rip off the whole facial mask.

Wishing to be, to act, to live. He must ask
First, in other words, to actually exist.

> And you, whiner, who wastes your time
>   Dawdling over the remorseless earth,
> What evil, what unspeakable crime
>   Have you made your life worth?

Inquest

Under the lamp your hands do not seem red.
What if the vicious histories didn't lie
And, in good time, might cover you with shame?—
You seldom hope to see yourself as dead.

How can you guess what vices on your head
Might shine like dead wood for some distant eye?
Of course you have your faults; you make no claim
To sainthood, but your hands do not look red.

It's no crime to be envied or well fed;
You aimed at no man's life. Who would deny
Yours is the human and the normal aim?
You scarcely want to see yourself as dead.

Only last week the commentators said
Not even foreign generals need die
For circumstantial crimes. You would proclaim
Your own guilt if you saw your own hands red.

If you were hungry, who'd give up his bread
Without a fight? A person has to try
To feed himself; earn his own wealth and fame;
Nobody wants to see himself as dead.

Still, men go back to wars. They're not misled
By the old lies. They know the reasons why.
When you can't praise the world your world became
And see no place where your own hands are red,

It must be someone, then—how have they fled
The justice you had hoped you could apply?
You've hanged your enemies, shown up their game,
So now you don't dare see yourself as dead

And things lose focus. You can lie in bed
Repeating Men do starve. Their children cry.
They really cry. They do not cry your name.
Go back to sleep, your hands do not feel red.

Or sit in some dark newsreel to be led
Through barbed wire and the white dead piled boot-high.
Your palms sweat; you feel just about the same.
Your last hope is to see yourself as dead

And yet you did not bleed when those were bled.
The humans carry knives. "It is not I!"
The screen goes blank, you see no one to blame.
Till you endure to see yourself as dead
Your blood in your own hands would not seem red.

A Flat One

Old Fritz, on this rotating bed
For seven wasted months you lay
Unfit to move, shrunken, gray,
No good to yourself or anyone
But to be babied—changed and bathed and fed.
    At long last, that's all done.

Before each meal, twice every night,
We set pads on your bedsores, shut
Your catheter tube off, then brought
The second canvas-and-black-iron
Bedframe and clamped you in between them, tight,
    Scared, so we could turn

You over. We washed you, covered you,
Cut up each bite of meat you ate;
We watched your lean jaws masticate
As ravenously your useless food
As thieves at hard labor in their chains chew
    Or insects in the wood.

Such pious sacrifice to give
You all you could demand of pain:
Receive this haddock's body, slain
For you, old tyrant; take this blood
Of a tomato, shed that you might live.
    You had that costly food.

You seem to be all finished, so
We'll plug your old recalcitrant anus
And tie up your discouraged penis
In a great, snow-white bow of gauze.
We wrap you, pin you, and cart you down below,
    Below, below, because

Your credit has finally run out.
On our steel table, trussed and carved,
You'll find this world's hardworking, starved
Teeth working in your precious skin.
The earth turns, in the end, by turn about
      And opens to take you in.

Seven months gone down the drain; thank God
That's through. Throw out the four-by-fours,
Swabsticks, the thick salve for bedsores,
Throw out the diaper pads and drug
Containers, pile the bedclothes in a wad,
      And rinse the cider jug

Half-filled with the last urine. Then
Empty out the cotton cans,
Autoclave the bowls and spit pans,
Unhook the pumps and all the red
Tubes—catheter, suction, oxygen;
      Next, wash the empty bed.

—All this Dark Age machinery
On which we had tormented you
To life. Last, we collect the few
Belongings: snapshots, some odd bills,
Your mail, and half a pack of Luckies we
      Won't light you after meals.

Old man, these seven months you've lain
Determined—not that you would live—
Just to not die. No one would give
You one chance you could ever wake
From that first night, much less go well again,
      Much less go home and make

Your living; how could you hope to find
A place for yourself in all creation?—
Pain was your only occupation.
And pain that should content and will
A man to give it up, nerved you to grind
        Your clenched teeth, breathing, till

Your skin broke down, your calves went flat
And your legs lost all sensation. Still,
You took enough morphine to kill
A strong man. Finally, nitrogen
Mustard: you could last two months after that;
        It would kill you then.

Even then you wouldn't quit.
Old soldier, yet you must have known
Inside the animal had grown
Sick of the world, made up its mind
To stop. Your mind ground on its separate
        Way, merciless and blind,

Into these last weeks when the breath
Would only come in fits and starts
That puffed out your sections like the parts
Of some enormous, damaged bug.
You waited, not for life, not for your death,
        Just for the deadening drug

That made your life seem bearable.
You still whispered you would not die.
Yet in the nights I heard you cry
Like a whipped child; in fierce old age
You whimpered, tears stood on your gun-metal
        Blue cheeks shaking with rage

And terror. So much pain would fill
Your room that when I left I'd pray
That if I came back the next day
I'd find you gone. You stayed for me—
Nailed to your own rapacious, stiff self-will.
          You've shook loose, finally.

They'd say this was a worthwhile job
Unless they tried it. It is mad
To throw our good lives after bad;
      Waste time, drugs, and our minds, while strong
Men starve. How many young men did we rob
          To keep you hanging on?

I can't think we did *you* much good.
Well, when you died, none of us wept.
You killed for us, and so we kept
You, because we need to earn our pay.
No. We'd still have to help you try. We would
          Have killed for you today.

Matisse: "The Red Studio"

There is no one here.
But the objects: they are real. It is not
As if he had stepped out or moved away;
There is no other room and no
Returning. Your foot or finger would pass
Through, as into unreflecting water
Red with clay, or into fire.
Still, the objects: they are real. It is
As if he had stood
Still in the bare center of this floor,
His mind turned in in concentrated fury,
Till he sank
Like a great beast sinking into sands
Slowly, and did not look up.
His own room drank him.
What else could generate this
Terra cotta raging through the floor and walls,
Through chests, chairs, the table and the clock,
Till all environments of living are
Transformed to energy—
Crude, definitive and gay.
And so gave birth to objects that are real.
How slowly they took shape, his children, here,
Grew solid and remain:
The crayons; these statues; the clear brandybowl;
The ashtray where a girl sleeps, curling among flowers;
This flask of tall glass, green, where a vine begins
Whose bines circle the other girl brown as a cypress knee.
Then, pictures, emerging on the walls:
Bathers; a landscape; a still life with a vase;
To the left, a golden blonde, lain in magentas with flowers
       scattering like stars;
Opposite, top right, these terra cotta women, living, in
       their world of living's colors;
Between, but yearning toward them, the sailor on his red
       café chair, dark blue, self-absorbed.

These stay, exact,
Within the belly of these walls that burn,
That must hum like the domed electric web
Within which, at the carnival, small cars bump and turn,
Toward which, for strength, they reach their iron hands:
Like the heavens' walls of flame that the old magi could see;
Or those ethereal clouds of energy
From which all constellations form,
Within whose love they turn.
They stand here real and ultimate.
But there is no one here.

Vuillard: "The Mother and Sister of the Artist"

(Instructions for the Visit)

Admire, when you come here, the glimmering hair
Of the girl; praise her pale
Complexion. Think well of her dress
Though that is somewhat out of fashion.
Don't try to take her hand, but smile for
Her hesitant gentleness.
Say the old woman is looking strong
Today; such hardiness. Remark,
Perhaps, how she has dressed herself black
Like a priest, and wears that sufficient air
That does become the righteous.
As you approach, she will push back
Her chair, shove away her plate
And wait,
Sitting squat and direct, before
The red mahogany chest
Massive as some great
Safe; will wait,
By the table and her greasy plate,
The bone half-chewed, her wine half-drained;
She will wait. And fix her steady
Eyes on you—the straight stare
Of an old politician.
Try once to meet her eyes. But fail.
Let your sight
Drift—yet never as if hunting for
The keys (you keep imagining) hung
By her belt. (They are not there.)
Watch, perhaps, that massive chest—the way
It tries to lean
Forward, toward her, till it seems to rest
Its whole household's weight

Of linens and clothing and provisions
All on her stiff back.
It might be strapped there like the monstrous pack
Of some enchanted pedlar. Dense, self-contained,
Like mercury in a ball,
She can support this without strain,
Yet she grows smaller, wrinkling
Like a potato, parched as dung;
It cramps her like a fist.
Ask no one why the chest
Has no knobs. Betray
No least suspicion
The necessities within
Could vanish at her
Will. Try not to think
That as she feeds, gains
Specific gravity,
She shrinks, light-
less as the world's
Hard core
And the per-
spective drains
In her.
Finally, above all,
You must not ever see,
Or let slip one hint you can see,
On the other side, the girl's
Cuffs, like cordovan restraints;
Forget her bony, tentative wrist,
The half-fed, worrying eyes, and how
She backs out, bows, and tries to bow
Out of the scene, grows too ethereal
To make a shape inside her dress

And the dress itself is beginning already
To sublime itself away like a vapor
That merges into the empty twinkling
Of the air and of the bright wallpaper.

Monet: "Les Nymphéas"

The eyelids glowing, some chill morning.
O world half-known through opening, twilit lids
   Before the vague face clenches into light;
O universal waters like a cloud,
   Like those first clouds of half-created matter;
O all things rising, rising like the fumes
   From waters falling, O forever falling;
Infinite, the skeletal shells that fall, relinquished,
   The snowsoft sift of the diatoms, like selves
Downdrifting age upon age through milky oceans;
   O slow downdrifting of the atoms;
O island nebulae and O the nebulous islands
   Wandering these mists like falsefires, which are true,
Bobbing like milkweed, like warm lanterns bobbing
   Through the snowfilled windless air, blinking and passing
As we pass into the memory of women
   Who are passing. Within those depths
What ravening? What devouring rage?
   How shall our living know its ends of yielding?
These things have taken me as the mouth an orange—
   That acrid sweet juice entering every cell;
And I am shared out. I become these things:
   These lilies, if these things are water lilies
Which are dancers growing dim across no floor;
   These mayflies; whirled dust orbiting in the sun;
This blossoming diffused as rushlights; galactic vapors;
   Fluorescence into which we pass and penetrate;
O soft as the thighs of women;
   O radiance, into which I go on dying . . .

Manet: "The Execution
of the Emperor Maximilian"

"Aim well, muchachos: aim right
here;" he pointed to his heart.
With face turned upward, he waited
grave but calm.

Dear good God, we've blundered into some musical
    Comedy; here we have the girls' *corps de ballet*
Got up as legionnaires and shooting several
    Supernumeraries. These dainty backs display
No strain lifting up and steadying rifles twice
    The length of those we use. True; their aim's not quite right.
What difference, though; their uniforms look so nice;
    The sabers in their white holsters all gleam so bright;
Their hats and spats and dress gear trim and orderly.
    They've worked hours to crease their pants, to shine buttons for
An event which—if you're a soldier—ought to be
    The peak of your career: to shoot an emperor!
One's shown up late, though—of course; to one side, he stands
    Coolly inspecting his rifle. Who knows, though—he
Maybe just gets bored with politics. Still, his hands
    Have just cocked the fate of nations. Wait, now; his cap's
Red; he doesn't wear spats—is he a sergeant, set
    To render the *coup de grace*? His face alone shows
Dignity and calm; he, above all, seems real. Yet
    Whether he has a name or purpose, no one knows.

A second volley was necessary for
Maximilian who had asked to be shot
in the chest so that his mother
might see his face.

The scumbly, half-formed heads of these few peons peak
    Up over the background which is a flat rock wall.
One yawns, one leans on his elbows, one rests his cheek
    On his crossed arms, drowsing. The others, meantime, sprawl
Around every which way like idlers who've gone numb
    With heat and flies watching some would-be matadors.
They look like angels bored with one more martyrdom.
    This one's not yawning, though—he's yelling. Still, of course,
That could mean triumph, hate, outrage or just shock. Who
    Knows? It could well be that he's waving to somebody
He knows—or just wants us to know he's here. We *do*
    Know him, after all: an old friend from Daumier's study
Of a mob rioting. So we can assume he
    Wants a revolt. Or. . . . wait; this face with the mantilla
And the fan—the classic Spanish temptress. What's she
    Doing here?—a high class lady straight out of Goya!
Meantime, along the wall, one hat's sneaking away
    At right, past our sergeant—or turned up late also.
One thing we *do* share with these peons—we can't say
    What they're doing here. This late, who will ever know?

                    On the spot where he died, the Haps-
                    burgs—whose general downfall was
                    prefigured in his—built a chapel
                    to further his remembrance on earth
                    and his forgiveness in heaven.

As for the victims, they would scarcely seem worth mention—
    Stuck in a corner, their whole world washed with flat light,
Focusless, having no perspective or convention
    To lead us in the way we ought to turn our sight.
At the center where the Emperor ought to stand, just
    This blank space rifles cross; otherwise, shadows thrown
In all directions; you'd think every man here must
    Have his inner light, like Quakers, or his own
Outer darkness. As if each flag flew in some thwart
    Direction, feeling a different wind. All the same,
For Maximilian, all aim and purpose stops short
    In this flat rock wall. Why speak of hints of cypress
Trees, shadowed lanes and cool vistas beyond the wall
    Far off at left? Out there, one white shape like a plaster
Bust drifts through the trees—a sort of neo-classical
    Ideal head floating, ghost-like, over the disaster.
Our hero stands as far from that as from this nameless
    Sergeant's real head, whose feet are well braced in the scene;
Untroubled, purposeless—he won't, for long, go aimless.
    He and stone walls are what men should not come between.

When Maximilian refused to believe the
absurd claim that he *had* been elected
by the peons, Napoleon threatened to
crown some other candidate. That, of
course, overcame all doubts.

Still, for Maximilian, he whose widow soon went
   Mad with loss—or with some love disease he'd brought
Her from Brazil—this "Lord of all the Firmament"
   As she always called him—this high-flown head that thought
All life one grand staircase at whose top he might stand
   Bestowing his smile of infinite grace upon
The human beings at its base, cannot command
   The central spot in its own execution.
Or the surest brush-work! This head with its fine dreams
   It could unite, somehow, the Old World with the New,
Bind the Divine Rights of Hapsburgs with half-baked schemes
   And liberal sentiments, could link the True Church to
The freely divisive mind, seems half-way divorced
   From its own body. Perched on a puff of smoke,
It bobs the way a kid's balloon slues back and forth
   At the end of its string. And, as a last bad joke,
Flaunts this broad sombrero—the tasteless parody
   Of a halo that may be fitting to a passion
Undergone between two generals. So we see
   Even gods must keep their heads and take note of fashions.

        It was as if some ne'er-do-well had
        finally found his true vocation: as
        martyr and sacrificial victim, he has
        seldom been surpassed.

Still, for Maximilian, he stands here holding hands
　　With these two who chose death with him. And that's about
All he held together. Now, even while he stands
　　Showing us the wounds in their palms, we've got our doubts.
He's bleached out like some child's two-penny crucifixion;
　　Even the eye wanders from that face where we see
Nothing of interest—not, surely, that firm conviction
　　We demand. After all, there's *some* nobility
In this unknown sergeant. Or in this general
　　At the rear, although he may seem hesitant to enter
The picture—as well he might. Wait, though; after all,
　　Maximilian might well have yielded up the center.
It could be this one, back of the others. Or else him,
　　In front, with legs spread, whose hand flaps up like a doll's,
The face nearly lost, yet twisting up in a dim
　　Shudder of strain—or, say, pain?—as the rifleballs
Break in and his brain cells, the atoms of his mind
　　Untie, all bonds dissolved they hurl free, first rats fleeing
The sinking vessel for some new faith, grasping, blind,
　　And he, whoever he was, is all done with being.

　　　1832: Birth, 6 July.
　　　1854: Naval adminstrator.
　　　1857: Viceroy to the Lombardo-Venetian Kingdom.
　　　1864: Emperor of Mexico.
　　　1867: Deposition; death.

Van Gogh: "The Starry Night"

Only the little
town
remains   beyond
all shock and dazzle
only this little
still stands
calm.

Row on row, the gray frame cottages, small
Barns and sheds of an old Dutch town;
Plane over plane, the village roofs in order,
One by one, contained and ordered lives;
Aging in place, the weathered walls gone
Gray, grown ancient beyond memory.

what flowers were blossoming, how the fruit
trees bore, had the nightingale been heard
yet, the text of Father's sermon

The squared shapes of doorframes, and bright windows;
Angle above angle, a slate ascent of roofs;
Stone upon stone, like broad stairs or the
Planes of a determined head, convergent
On this still dead center, the village chapel
Tiny as a child's toy

There is something about Father
narrow-minded, icy-cold, like iron

The village chapel, tiny as a child's toy
And as far. Pale as quartz crystals,
Its salients and the keen blue spire
Slim as a needle transfixed in the horizon
Firm in the high winds, high breakers, this
Still eye to the hurricane, this lighthouse

> *How could I possibly be in any way of any*
> *use to anyone? I am good for something!*

In which no light shines.

Through the high zones uncontained
          the uncontaining heavens
     Metaphysics cannot hold
          hump shove swirling blood rising as
     the nipples too come swollen shuddery
               behind the clenched lids, blind
tracers   *chaos in a goblet*   opening
     like a zinnia bed   and chancres   swamp mouths
               outspattering eleven
          fixed stars   one sunburst moon
     Midspasm   midheavens   the spiral galaxy
          tumbled in trails of vapor
               Art for Art
          The war still raging while the high gods
     copulate on Garganos
               the holy ground burst
          into flower and a golden dew fell

Energy for Energy
ethereal first mists   light dusts
        Chaos contains no glass
         of our caliber
gathering into force and matter
      obliterating to be whole again
    be one.

       Giotto and Cimabue live in an obeliscal
       society, solidly framed, architecturally constructed.

Row on row, plane over plane, the reddish brown
Houses with stepped gables and high stoops.
One by one, the thoughtless comfortable lives
Like steps in an argument, pigs at their dam;
Side by side in one another's lee, huddled
Against weather, against doubt, passion, hope

       Every individual a stone and
       the stones clung together

The narrow lanes beneath the eaves-troughs,
Hedgerows between the houses and dark
Trees; behind, and laid out side by side,
The kitchen gardens with their heavy odors
Where dew sits chilly on the cabbage leaves
And a bird might sing.

       And if no actual obelisk of too
       pyramidal a tragedy, no rain of frogs

Down those dark lanes you will never see
A lantern move or any shadow sway,
No dog howl and your ear will never know
The footfall of a prowler or some lover's tread,
Nor any wanderer, long gone,

*four great crises when I did not know what
I said, what I wanted, even what I did.*

who cannot return.

*In spring, a caged bird feels strongly
there is something he should be doing.
But what was it? He gets vague ideas.
The children say, but he has everything
he wants.*

Beyond the town, blue mountains rising
    range over range over range
*Sometimes just as waves break
    on sullen, hopeless cliffs*
               upthrusting
      its salt mass into the sky
in the public square milling chanting obscenities
          ton on broken ton of stone
      the black earth hovering *I feel a
        storm of desire to
          embrace something*
great ragged crests lumbering in   murderous
   as the seasons   bluer than the years
      the first rocks rattling
through the windows   scattered gunfire
     all you have always held is a lie

Painting   and much screwing are not
      compatible; man   the crowd
      pounds   on and on   blood battering its walls
the feathery surf   first spies   already
            prowling up around the gray
      outbuildings and the orchards
            the unthinkable is also true
                        becomes ambitious as soon
      as he becomes impotent a spume
of ancient vacuum shuddering to
            reclaim its child
to embrace   something   a woman   a sort
      of domestic hen
            so pale
the gardens of olives   gardens
      of agony   frothing
            about its feet in foam.

                  the hollow dreams of revolutionaries . . .
                  they would wail in despair if once they
                  forgot the easy satisfaction of their
                  instincts, raising them to the unappeased
                  sufferings of the passions.

Down those dark lanes which you can never see
      Shines only so much light:
Eleven windows and one opened door—crystals
      Under tons of ore, clear garnets, warm;
Through those windows you can never see, and yet
      You always wonder who may waken there,

Who sits up late over a pipe, sits to hold
   A pious, worn book between worn hands,
Who sits up late together and will talk, will talk
   The night away, planning the garden for
Next year, the necessary furnitures,
   Who works there, shreds the cabbages,
Darns some coarse fabric by a hanging lamp,
   Who may have gotten out of bed to calm
Their children fitfully sleeping, each
   In his own bed, one by one another,
Who goes to curry and bed down the patient beasts
   Warm in their old pens. But nothing moves
In those dark streets which you can never see,
   No one is walking or will ever walk there
Now, and you will never know

                One vast tree
            between you and the town:
               one cypress   mocks
            the thin blue spire   licking up
                    like flame
                        the green metabolism
               of this forest sword
            driving you from the town

            I have sown a little garden of poppies,
            sweet peas and mignonette. Now we must
            wait and see what comes of it.

Still, though the little town, how peacefully
It lies under the watchful eyes of that
Fierce heaven.

We take death to reach a star.

Nothing moves there yet, and yet
How separate, how floating like a raft, like
Seaweed drifting outward on the tide, already
Dim, half-gone,

*And the poor baby, too, whom I had
cared for as if he were my own*

diminishing into
Some middle distance of the past.

*some canvases that will retain their
calm even in the catastrophe*

and still so calm
and still
so still

Zóó heen kan gaan

The
Fuehrer Bunker

Even if we lose this war, we still win, for our spirit will have penetrated the hearts of our enemies.

—Joseph Goebbels

Mother Theresa, asked when she first began her work of relief and care for abandoned children, replied, "On the day I discovered I had a Hitler inside me."

Dr. Joseph Goebbels
Minister for Propaganda

—1 April 1945, 0230 hours

> *(At a French window of his house on
> Schwanenwerder, he watches the air
> raid over Berlin. He sings snatches of a
> song from the Thirty Years War.)*

By day, American bomb flights
Smash us to ash and brick dust; nights,
The British burn us down. Up there,
Not one of our planes anywhere.
Revive, rise, you Powers of the Air—
It's Easter! Ha!—we haven't got a prayer!

Pray, children, pray;
Swedes are on the way.

So "Red Berlin" burns—turning red
Once more. Those same streets piled with dead
Where we once cracked men's skulls to win
Their hearts and high offices. Once in,
We swore we'd never leave except
Feet first—that's one promise we've kept.
We did neglect to tell them, though:
Let this earth tremble when we go!

Oxenstiern will march this way
Teaching children how to pray.

> *(turns from the window)*

The first time I saw a bombed city—
Dresden—corrupted me with pity.
Some suffocated, others burned
Alive; some, lacking air, turned
Black and hard—their body fats ran
Out of them like grease in a pan.

Then he'll roast the fat, young pullets;
Melt church windows down for bullets.

I clumped through those long stacks of dead
Weeping, weeping. Back here, I said
I wanted power right then for putting
This whole nation on a war footing.
Now the foe's halfway through our gate
The Chief gives me the power. Too late.

Bet, kinder, bet;

So once more, the Chief's wrong proves out
Better than my right. I, no doubt,
Could have curbed slaughter, ruin, terror—
Just my old sentimental error.
Our role is to wipe out a twisted
Life that should never have existed.

Morgen komm der Schwed.

Each Ami bomb, each Russian shell
Helps us to wipe away this hell
Called Europe, Man's age-old, unjust
Network of lies, pandering, lust,
Deformity. This is to be
Young again—idealistic, free.

Morgen komm der Oxenstierne

Once, my newscasters would disguise
Each loss as a triumph. Those lies
Were mere truths *we* misunderstood:
There's no evil we can't find good.

Will der kinder beten lerne.

    (turns back to the window)

Let it all fall in, burn and burst;
Blest be who dares act out his worst
Impulses, give way to the thirst
For blood, and show this for the accurst
Inferno we took it for, right from the first.

Bet, kinder, bet.
Pray, children, pray.

(kneels)

Our Father who art in Nihil,
We thank Thee for this day of trial
And for the loss that teaches self-denial.
Amen.

Reichsmarschall Hermann Göring

—1 April 1945

*(Göring, head of the Luftwaffe, once
bragged that if one German city were
bombed, they could call him "Meier."
At his Karinhall estate, he questions
himself and his disgrace.)*

And why, Herr Reichsmarschall, is Italy
Just like schnitzel? *If they're beaten
Either one will just get bigger.
Neither cuts too firm a figure.*
Still, all this humble pie you've eaten
Lately, fills you out quite prettily.

Why then, Herr Göring, how can we
Tell you and Italy apart?
*Italy always wins through losing;
I, just the opposite, by using
High skills and cunning, learned the art
Of flat pratfalls through victory.*

You've led our Flying Circus; how
Could our war ace turn to a clown?
*Both pad out over-extended fronts;
Both keep alive doing slick stunts
And, even so, both get shot down.*
But only one's called "Meier" now.

Pray, could an old, soft football be
Much like a man in deep disgrace?
*They don't kick back; don't even dare
Look up—the British own the air!*
Then, stick a needle in someplace;
Pump yourself full of vacancy.

129

Tell us, dear Minister for Air,
Are warriors, then, like a bad smell?
Neither stays inside its borders;
Either's bound to follow ordures;
They both expand and play the swell
Though something's getting spoiled somewhere.

Then answer one more question, which is
Are politicians like whipped cream?
They both inflate themselves with gas;
Also they both puff up your ass
Till you're exposed like some bad dream
Where you've grown too big for your britches.

Herr President, can't we tell apart
An artful statesman and an ass?
Fat chance! One spouts out high ideals;
One makes low rumblings after meals.
But that's the threat of leaking gas
Which all men fear! *No; that's a fart.*

Last, could you give one simple rule
To tell a medal from a turd?
No. They both come from those above you
Conveying their opinion of you.
Right! Here's your new medal, conferred
For vast achievements: April Fool!

(Himmler's ruthless extermination policies were based on fantastic pseudoscientific experiments and theories. MM=74.)

ANY · TRULY · MODERN · STUDY · OF · THE ·
BRAIN · MUST · COOLLY · METHODICALLY
CONSIDER · THE · RACES · PROGRESS · & ·
DEVELOPMENT · WE · MUST · MAKE · EVERY
EFFORT · TO · ISOLATE · THE · CRUCIAL ·

FACTORS · THAT · MAKE · SOME · PEOPLES
GREAT · WHILE · OTHERS · DEGENERATE ·
HUMANITY · CANNOT · AFFORD · TO · WAIT
IVE · HAD · MY · MEN · GATHER · 1000S · OF
JEWISH · SKULLS · WE · MEASURE · WEIGH

KEEP · COMPLETE · RECORDS · & · BEFORE
LONG · CAN · HOPE · TO · UNRAVEL · THIS ·
MYSTERY · ABOVE · ALL · ELSE · DEVOTED
NAZIS · MUST · KEEP · A · SCIENTIFIC · &
OBJECTIVE · VIEW · IF · WE · WANT · REAL

PROGRESS · I · HAVE · BEEN · STUDYING ·
QUITE · THOROUGHLY · OUR · DARK · AGES
RECORDS · SHOW · 1000S · WENT · TO · THE
STAKE · PEOPLE · HONESTLY · BELIEVED
THEM · TO · BE · WITCHES · ITS · SIMPLY ·

UNTHINKABLE · MONSTROUS · WASTING ·
VALUABLE · GERMAN · BLOOD · TO · BURN ·
WITCHES · THAT · JUST · GOES · TO · SHOW
YOU · WHAT · FOLLY · & · INSANE · EXCESS
ZEALOTS · & · FANATICS · CAN · FALL · TO

131

ALL·OUR·WORK·IS·ENDANGERED·NOW
BY·THIS·BARBAROUS·ONSLAUGHT·OF
COMMUNISTIC·HORDES·SINCE·SUCH·
DUMB·HALF-CIVILIZED·BRUTES·ARE
ENEMIES·OF·TRUE·CULTURE·&·THE·

FULLY·RATIONAL·MIND·SO·WE·MUST
GATHER·ALL·RECORDS·ALL·REMAINS
HIDE·ANY·EVIDENCE·WHICH·COULD·
INDICATE·WHAT·WEVE·DONE·THATS·
JUST·AS·VITAL·NOW·AS·IT·IS·TO·

KEEP·THE·CAMPS·SWEPT·CLEAN·ALL
LABORATORIES·MUST·BE·TORN·DOWN
MOVED·OR·THOROUGHLY·DISGUISED·
NEW·TITLES·SHOULD·BE·ISSUED·TO
OUR·DOCTORS·AND·TECHNICIANS·I·

PALE·TO·THINK·WHAT·THEY·WOULD·
QUITE·POSSIBLY·IMAGINE·IF·THEY
ROOTED·INTO·OUR·MASS·GRAVES·OR
SOME·OF·OUR·BOLDER·EXPERIMENTS
THEYD·MISUNDERSTAND·IT·CALL·US

UNPRINCIPLED·HOODLUMS·GIVEN·TO
VICIOUS·INSTINCTS·THEYD·CLAIM·
WE·HAD·LOST·ALL·CONSCIENCE·AND
YIELDED·TO·THE·WORSHIP·OF·BAAL
ZOROASTER·SOMETHING·IRRATIONAL

Adolf Hitler

—20 April 1945, 1900 hours

*(After his birthday ceremony, Hitler
has withdrawn to his sitting room
where he sits with one of Blondi's
puppies on his knee. Earlier in the
day he had gone up into the garden
for the last time.)*

Better stuffed in a bag; drowned.
My best bitch pregnant once she can't
Survive.

The man will lie down on his back; his partner crouches over his
head or chest as he prefers.

My Effie's little sister
Knocked up by Fegelein. My luck
Lets me off one humiliation:
I breed no child.

He, of course, is completely naked.

This mockery:
Pisspot generals whining for surrender;
Party maggots bringing presents;
Careful not to wish me a long life—
Their one failure I can share.
Pulling at me, whimpering for
Their cities, populations, lives.

Sometimes, she may remove only her underthings. The private
parts, suddenly exposed, can provide an exquisite shock and
pleasure.

Cub, in Landsberg Prison, after
Our first putsch failed, my flowers
Filled three prison rooms. The faithful
Sang beside me in my cell.
I unwrapped presents, cut my cake. We
Laughed: where was the file inside?

The cake my mother made me . . . No . . .

Usually she will turn her back.

No. That's Edmund's cake. My brother's.
But I ate Edmund's cake. I spit on
What was left.

The Prison Governor brought his family's
Kind regards. His little daughter curled up,
Like this, on my lap asleep.

She must not start at once; he must ask, even beg her, to begin.

Whimpering at me; whining. Oh,
We hear their song:

Only live. Live longer. Lead us
To the mountain fastnesses. Keep us
From the guns, the Russians . . .

"Oh stay! don't leave us here forsaken;
Our men are waiting for their Führer."

134

In the mountains, could these shitheads be
Worthwhile? Over and over, we've said
They could survive: overcome facts.

Today I climbed two flights to the garden:
Sour smoke. Shelling. Schoolboys lined up.
Lines of graves. Hands I have to touch.

He will grovel on the floor, declaring himself unworthy to touch
her shoes, even to live.

Even the zoo animals, my good old
Neighbors, pacing their stalls till
Their keeper brings the right gift—
One lead pellet. A man who would accept
What is, is criminal, too vile to live.

It is not the mere fact of the urine or the feces that is significant.
The crux is that he be able to watch these emerge into existence.

Suffer that again? The elevator
Locked, lurching up through dead rock
In the mountain side? Come out
Freezing, over the receding plains,
Traitorous cities, nauseous dens
And hovels, lecherous faces with insane
Beliefs, Czechs, Jews with blond hair,
Blue eyes, who would steal our birthright,
Pull us down into putrescence, slime?

Edmund died though, my brother,
When I was eleven. His birthday
Would have been some days ago.

She must now show disgust; may revile him, even kick at him.

She lost three others. She, only
She, was glad I had survived.

Only when he is fully excited by his own demands, may she
release her urine, open her bowels. The danger of taking this
matter in his mouth heightens the excitement.

Only live; live longer. Don't
Leave us to the loneliness,
The spoiling of affections.

He kept me in. But she,
She made a special cake for me—
Only the two of us together.

Now he will probably achieve his climax, alone and without
assistance.

Namesake, cub, you've done your month
In this filth. My cake; I'll eat it, too.

The First War soldiers; our Old Fighters—
That was comradeship. You have Blondi's
Underside; my diet cook, the drivers,
Secretaries—they know how to listen.

"𝕴 stay too long; the 𝕲rail has sent for me."

I can eat nothing now—only cake.
Pills and Morrell's injections.
My cake, chairs, rugs—without them,
There's the bare concrete. Like any
Jew degenerate at Auschwitz.

When he has washed and begged forgiveness, she may embrace
and comfort him.

My birthday present, my file: my
Cartridge of pure cyanide. Crawl back
In the cave, work down in dry leaves,
An old dog deciding to lie down.

Or she may curl up by his side.

Eva Braun

—22 April 1945

*(Hitler's mistress received no public
recognition and often felt badly
neglected. Her small revenges included
singing American songs, her favorite
being "Tea for Two." Having chosen
to die with him in the bunker, she
appeared quite serene during the
last days.)*

*Tea for two
And two for tea*

        I ought to feel ashamed
Feeling such joy. Behaving like a spoiled child!
So fulfilled. This is a very serious matter.
All of them have come here to die. And they grieve.
I have come here to die. If this is dying,
Why else did I ever live?

*Me for you
And you for me*

We ought never to flaunt our good luck
In the face of anyone less fortunate—
These live fools mourning already
For their own deaths; these dead fools
Who believe they can go on living . . ,

*And you for me
Alone.*

Who out of all of them, officers, ministers,
These liars that despise me, these empty
Women that envy me—so they hate me—
Who else of them dares to disobey Him
As I dared? I have defied Him to His face
And He has honored me.

> We *will raise*
> A *family*

They sneer at me—at my worrying about
Frau Goebbels' children, that I make fairytales
For them, that we play at war. Is our war
More lost if I console these poor trapped rabbits?
These children He would not give me . . .

A boy for you
A girl for me

They sneer that I should bring
Fine furniture down this dank hole. Speer
Built this bed for me. Where I have slept
Beside our Chief. Who else should have it?
My furs, my best dress to my little sister—
They would sneer even at this; yet
What else can I give her?

> *Can't you see*
> *How happy we would be?*

                              Or to the baby
         She will bear Fegelein? Lechering dolt!
         Well, I have given her her wedding
         As if it was my own. And she will have
         My diamonds, my watch. The little things you
         Count on, things that see you through your
         Missing life, the life that stood you up.

   Nobody near us
   To see us or hear us

         I have it all. They are all gone, the others—
         The Valkyrie, and the old rich bitch Bechstein;
         Geli above all. No, the screaming mobs above all.
         They are all gone now; He has left them all.
         No one but me and the love-struck secretaries—
         Traudl, Daran—who gave up years ago.

                              No friends or relations
                              On weekend vacations

         That I, I above all, am chosen—even I
         Must find that strange. I who was always
         Disobedient, rebellious—smoked in the dining car,
         Wore rouge whenever he said I shouldn't.
         When he ordered that poor Chancellor Schuschnigg
         Was to starve, I sent in food.

   We won't have it known, dear,
   That we own a telephone, dear.

I who joined the Party, I who took Him
For my lover just to spite my old stiff father—
Den Alten Fritz—and those stupid nuns.
I ran my teachers crazy, and my mother—I
Held out even when she stuck my head in water.
He shall have none but me.

Day will break
And you will wake

We cannot make it through another month;
We follow the battles now on a subway map.
Even if the Russians pulled back—
His hand trembles, the whole left side
Staggers. His marvelous eyes are failing.
We go out to the sunlight less each day. We live
Like flies sucked up in a sweeper bag.

And start to bake
A sugar cake

He forbade me to leave Berchtesgaden,
Forbade me to come here. I tricked
My keepers, stole my own car, my driver Jung.
He tried to scold me; He was too
Proud of me. Today He ordered me to leave,
To go back to the mountain. I refused.
I have refused to save my own life and He,
In public, He kissed me on the mouth.

141

For me to take
For all the boys to see.

Once more I have won, won out over Him
Who spoke one word and whole populations vanished.
Until today, in public, we were good friends.
He is mine. No doubt
I did only what He wanted; no doubt
I should resent that. In the face
Of such fulfillment? In the face
Of so much joy?

Picture you
Upon my knee;
Tea for two
And two for tea . . .

Dr. Joseph Goebbels

—22 April 1945

*(On this date, Goebbels moved into the
lowest level of the bunker, taking a
room opposite Hitler's.)*

Stand back, make way, you mindless scum,
Squire Voland the Seducer's come—
Old Bock from Babelsberg whose tower
Falls silent now, whose shrunken power
For lies or lays comes hobbling home
Into this concrete catacomb.

Here's Runty Joe, the cunt collector
Who grew to greatness, first erector
Of myths and missions, fibs and fables,
Who pulled the wool then turned the tables:
He piped the tunes and called the dance
Where shirtless countries lost their pants.

Goatfooted Pan, the nation's gander
To whom Pan-Germans all played pander,
The jovial cob-swan quick to cover
Lida Baarova, his check-list lover;
Swellfoot the Tyrant, he could riddle
Men's minds away, hi-diddle-diddle.

Our little Doctor, Joe the Gimp
Comes back to limpness and his limp:
Hephaistos, Vulcan the lame smith
Whose net of lies caught one true myth:
His wife, the famous beauty, whored
By numbskull Mars, the dull warlord.

What if I took my little fling
At conquest, at adventuring.
Pried the lid of Pandora's box off—
There's nothing there to bring your rocks off.
I never saw one fucking day
So fine I courted it to stay.

If I got snarled in my own mesh
Of thighs and bellies, who wants flesh?
I never hankered after matter.
Let Hermann swell up, grosser, fatter,
Weighed down by medals, houses, clothing;
They leave me lean, secured in loathing.

As a young man, I pricked the bubble
Of every creed; I saw that rubble
And offered myself the realms of earth
Just to say Yes. But what's it worth?
No thank you, Ma'am. Behold the Ram
Of God: I doubt, therefore I am.

Here I forsake that long pricktease
Of histories, hopes, lusts, luxuries.
I come back to my first Ideal—
The vacancy that's always real.
I sniffed out all life's openings:
I loved only the holes in things.

So strip down one bare cell for this
Lay Brother of the last abyss.
To me, still, all abstractions smell;
My head and nose clear in this cell
Of concrete, this confession booth
Where liars face up to blank truth.

My tongue lashed millions to the knife;
Here, I'll hold hands with my soiled wife.
My lies piped men out, hot to slaughter;
Here, I'll read stories to my daughter
Then hack off all relations, choose
Only the Nothing you can't lose,

Send back this body, fixed in its
Infantile paralysis.
I was born small; I shall grow less
Till I burst into Nothingness,
That slot in time where only pure
Spirit extends, absent and sure.

I am that spirit that denies,
High Priest of Laymen, Prince of Lies.
Your house is founded on my rock;
Truth crows; now I deny my cock.
Jock of this walk, I turn down all,
Robbing my Peter to play Paul.

I give up all goods I possess
To build my faith on faithlessness.
Black Peter, I belie my Lord—
You've got to die to spread the Word.
Now the last act; there's no sequel.
Soon, once more, all things shall be equal.

Magda Goebbels

—22 April 1945

*(On this date, Magda and her six
children by Goebbels moved into the
upper level of the bunker.)*

i

How could you dare stay constant to
The kind that kept their faith to me?
   They hang on; they need help from you.
How could you dare stay constant to
   Those who can't help you struggle through;
   What use could such poor weaklings be?
How could you dare stay constant to
The kind that kept their faith to me?

ii

Who could you give devotion to?
Those that treat you faithlessly.
   On all sides, this world threatens you;
Who could you give devotion to?
   The strong; they don't care what they do;
   They tramp down all bounds, then go free.
Who could you give devotion to?
Those that treat you faithlessly.

iii

You raise your child devotedly;
He grows strong, then goes his own way.
   How helpless you must seem to be.
You raise your child devotedly
   And that tells him you need him; he
   Sees no real reason not to stray.
You raise your child devotedly;
He grows strong, then goes his own way.

iv

What can you do but turn away?
They'll see you're strong, then; they'll stay true.
    We've seen what loyalties would pay.
What can you do but turn away
    So that they'll need you. *Now* they'll stay
    Too scared to break their ties with you.
What can you do but turn away?
They'll see you're strong, then; they'll stay true.

Reichsmarschall Hermann Göring

—23 April 1945

*(After the conference of April 20,
Hitler's birthday, Göring drove south to
Berchtesgaden with a convoy of forty
vehicles. Having set up headquarters
there, he imagines the splendors of his
erstwhile parties.)*

Dear friends, the moment's come to ask
What lies beneath the glittering gear
And costumes radiantly displayed
At the Reichsmarschall's masquerade;
Find who romanced and danced us here,
To face the face behind the mask.

Who can adapt to each new role
And change costumes so cunningly
With each day's new conditions that
He wears a lantern on his hat
When he must run downstairs to see
The man who comes delivering coal?

Whose self-made uniform asserts
Clear blue, horizon to horizon,
Like azure skies no enemy
Dares invade; where instead we see
Medals like close-drilled stars bedizen
An ever-expanding universe?

Who wears this tent-sized dressing gown
All day, bought forty business suits
So he could change each hour or two
For fear his sour sweat might soak through?
Is this our famous Puss-in-Boots
Or just some knock-down, drag-out clown?

Who steps up now to the forefront
Wearing this pair of lederhosen,
A dagger tucked in his wide belt
And rough-cut vest from a deer's pelt
To signify himself the chosen
Chief of Reich Forests and the Hunt.

Who flaunts this frilly satin blouse,
These velvet knickerbockers, that
Alluring jacket of green suede
And in such fluff and frou-frou played
The true effete aristocrat,
The idle lord of an old house?

Who wears this modern well-ironed version
Of a toga he must hope dangles
Over his circular abdomen
Like an Athenian lord or Roman,
But with his nail paint, rouge and bangles
Looks more like some debauched Persian?

Who, at the Fuehrer's staff confab,
Accused of crimes just short of treason,
Got Hitler's leave to flee Berlin
And drive south, while he stood there in
The smartest fashion note this season:
Garb of American olive-drab?

Who wears this thick flesh, layer on layer—
Loose outposts of a weakening heart?
Who seems a one-man population
Explosion, or expanding nation,
Then, at the showdown, gives you a start:
He lifts his mask and no one's there.

HEINRICH · HIMMLER
FORMER · REICHSFUEHRER · SS
—29 · APRIL · 1945 ·

(After his secret negotiations for surrender to the West were revealed, Himmler was declared a traitor and expelled from the party by Hitler. MM=80.)

```
A · WISE · MAN · ALWAYS · KNOWS · HE · MAY
BE · MISUNDERSTOOD · REVILED · TO · BE
CALLED · A · TRAITOR · WHEN · I · MERELY
DID · MY · BEST · TO · SAVE · OUR · TROOPS
EVEN · SAVE · HIS · OWN · LIFE · WITH · MY

FOREIGN · CONTACTS · ALSO · USING · MY
GOOD · NAME · AFTER · LONG · YEARS · OF ·
HONORABLE · SERVICE · & · HARDSHIPS ·
I · BORE · FOR · HIM · GETTING · RID · OF ·
JEWS · GYPSIES · YOUD · THINK · I · LIKE

KILLING · ALL · THOSE · PEOPLE · O · ITS
LITTLE · THANKS · YOU · GET · BESIDES ·
MY · STOMACH · CRAMPS · TRULY · THERES
NO · JUSTICE · TRUE · I · DIDNT · DO · IT ·
ORIGINALLY · JUST · FOR · IDEALISTIC

PURPOSES · I · COULD · HAVE · MADE · IT ·
QUITE · IDEALISTIC · LATER · ON · AND ·
REALLY · NOW · TO · KILL · THAT · MANY · &
STAY · DECENT · UPRIGHT · IDEALISTIC
THAT · DESERVES · SOMETHING · I · GAVE

UP · MY · HAPPY · CHICKEN · FARM · & · THE
VICIOUS · THINGS · THEY · CALLED · ME ·
WHY · I · FAINT · JUST · SEEING · BLOOD ·
YET · HARD · AS · IT · IS · WE · MUST · KEEP
ZEAL · MORALITY · & · SELF - SACRIFICE
```

152

Eva Ƀ Hitler, geb. Braun

—30 April 1945

*(After her improvised civil wedding
and the brief reception, Eva sits on the
bed in her room alone. Hitler has gone
with Traudl Junge, his secretary, to
dictate his will before their mutual
deaths in a few hours. Fragments of
the Mass and the formal Catholic
marriage service run through her
mind.)*

Consummatum est.

It is accomplishèd.
    My mother's will be done.
               Is done.

      The Dodd Girl, the Valkyrie,
    Ley's wife, Geli above all—
      how many died
so I could carry her
    His name. When we were kids
      we looked at the eclipse
through snapshot negatives. They held
    their longing up to Him; their sight
      flashed out. Twice
I tried to kill myself.

*To Thee do we cry, poor banished
children of Eve.*

153

At the photographer's I called Him
"Herr Wolf"; we met
disguised. Later,
He'd slip me an envelope
with enough to live on. Never
a love note; never a word
in public. I sat at my dresser
kissing His picture through glass;
in April weather, the sun
outside my windows
sneered at me. We drove
to the Munich Station; His train
had gone; all we saw
was tail lights. He
was never there. Only my first "suicide"
brought Him in. Tonight
the third. This one
for dead sure.

What God hath joined together
let no man put asunder.

A boy, He wouldn't listen
to the priest; they'd find Him
catching sunlight
in a pocket mirror, playing it
around the trees, the courtyard. Even now
He has gone off with Traudl
to dictate His will. Since He cannot
have His will. He leaves me
this concession
I once was:
my crossed-out name, my
new name on a piece of paper:
Eva ƀ Hitler, geb. Braun.

Therefore shall a man leave father
and mother and cleave to his wife.
They shall be one flesh.

And even if He came, He
would be missing; He
would not hear me. I
could look through Him
like a worn-out lantern slide. The priest
held up the monstrance
they said held the Host
before the people, right and left,
while we cast down our eyes. But one day I
crept up in the empty chapel,
to the holy case. There
the sacred vestments, the gold
chains, the monstrance
rayed out gleaming
like the May sun. And in the
center, the tiny glass bead,
I could see nothing.
Nothing.

And yet I have these albums, these
pictures proving it all so.
We danced together; we
sat together over tea; even
the wedding ceremony . . .
My grandmother's brocade—
I left it at the mountain;
I had to wear my long black taffeta.
This ring delivered for me
by the Gestapo . . .
I am black but beautiful
ye daughters of Jerusalem.

With this ring I thee wed;
This gold and silver I thee bring.

. . . this ring torn off some Jew's hand.

in templo sancto tuo in Jerusalem.

I am the Black Bride that will be
devoured, that will pass
down into Him like used water
down a drain, a film stuck,
burning through, or reeling
back into itself.
Like all the women, all
the foreigners, our beautiful
young men—all small
as red ants under
the magnifying glass
He reads His maps by.

Consummatum est.

To be so soon consumed and
never consummated.

O Thou who hast created
all things out of nothing . . .

157

Now each one has the nothing
they fought for. We have earned
our deaths. And yet,
my mother, not even she
would will me this. She only wants
it all to mean
her meaning. Something instead
of life. To tell the neighbors.
And that I give her. She
can rest.

Ite. Missa est.

My mother's will be mine.
Is
mine.

It is accomplishèd.

Adolf Hitler

—30 April 1945, 1520 hours

> *(Russian troops are in Voss and*
> *Wilhelm Strasse. Hitler and Eva have*
> *withdrawn to his sitting room; she has*
> *already committed suicide.)*

More than fifty millions. More.
Who killed that much; who else?

    Russian: twenty million.
    Jew: seven million, five hundred thousand.

        "Casualties can never be high enough.
        They are the seeds of future heroism."

All that and what good: what does
That save you? On and on and on . . .

Traitors on every side! Lies! Lies!

One gift, finally, to my faithful:
At Attila's bier. Last night,
My secretaries, cook, the short-wave girls.
More potent than bull-sperm; one cartridge
Each. A helping hand, to save you
From these Mongolians' greasy hands,
Pricks, the stink of jism. What then?
Some will sneak off West; some
Wait till the Russian tanks . . . overcome
By their own lust . . .

"𝔅𝔢𝔱𝔯𝔞𝔶𝔢𝔡! 𝔅𝔢𝔱𝔯𝔞𝔶𝔢𝔡! 𝔖𝔥𝔞𝔪𝔢𝔣𝔲𝔩𝔩𝔶 𝔟𝔢𝔱𝔯𝔞𝔶𝔢𝔡!
𝔇𝔢𝔠𝔢𝔦𝔱! 𝔇𝔢𝔠𝔢𝔦𝔱! 𝔏𝔶𝔦𝔫𝔤 𝔭𝔞𝔰𝔱 𝔞𝔩𝔩 𝔯𝔢𝔳𝔢𝔫𝔤𝔢!"

Pole: three million.

          "Casualties? But that's what
          the young men are there for."

And seven at one blow.

Again last night, our movie:
Witzleben. General Joke Life. Choke Alive.
Shriveled-up rat, hauled up, wriggling
On the meat-hook, handcuffed, naked,
Six times to choke and strangle. Five times
Hauled down. Brought back. Couldn't
Beg even to die. Not even. Scrawny
Pizzle wouldn't come again. Not dust.
He couldn't even . . .

          I bring you not peace but
          a sword. This death in honor.

     Gypsy: four hundred . . . four . . .
        four hundred thousand.

      Not one truly grateful.

      French: five hundred thousand.

Shoveling lime in a latrine. Oh,
It's dragon seed. We played it three times;
No satisfaction. Not even . . .

Jugoslav: five hundred . . .

What use are facts, statistics?
The Impossible always succeeds.
Will enough and the lie turns true.

German: spineless worms. Only four . . .
four hundred . . . only four . . .

(turns to Eva's body)

Not even this one. Not even then.
She chose. Not watching her. Even
To come here was insulting. Mortal.

"𝕺nce recognized, the 𝕲rail 𝕶night must be gone."

Betrayed to! Lies! Betrayed to!

Never to need anyone alive. Whose
Death gets you through? Whose death
Shows you more fit to live? Whose . . .

Who's afraid of the big bad wolf,
Ha-ha-ha-ha-ha!

Tell me I have to die, then. Tell me.
What have I counted on? Tell me
The odds against me. You can't be
Sure enough. My name. My name on
Every calendar. Relentless, each year,
Your birth comes around. My death:
My lackey; my lickass general. My Will
Scrubs it all out, all of you, all gone . . .

"I go with the precision and
security of a sleepwalker."

I pick my time, my place. I take
This capsule tight between my teeth . . .
Set this steel cold against my jaw . . .
Clench, clench . . . and once more I
Am winning,
        winning,
                winning . . .

Magda Goebbels

—30 April 1945

*(After Dr. Haase gave them shots of
morphine, Magda gave each child an
ampule of potassium cyanide from a
spoon.)*

This is the needle that we give
Soldiers and children when they live
Near the front in primitive
   Conditions or real dangers;
This is the spoon we use to feed
Men trapped in trouble or in need,
When weakness or bad luck might lead
   Them to the hands of strangers.

This is the room where you can sleep
Your sleep out, curled up under deep
Layers of covering that will keep
   You safe till all harm's past.
This is the bed where you can rest
In perfect silence, undistressed
By noise or nightmares, as my breast
   Once held you soft but fast.

This is the Doctor who has brought
Your needle with your special shot
To quiet you; you won't get caught
   Off guard or unprepared.
I am your nurse who'll comfort you;
I nursed you, fed you till you grew
Too big to feed; now you're all through
   Fretting or feeling scared.

This is the glass tube that contains
Calm that will spread down through your veins
To free you finally from all pains
    Of going on in error.
This tiny pinprick sets the germ
Inside you that fills out its term
Till you can feel yourself grow firm
    Against all doubt, all terror.

Into this spoon I break the pill
That stiffens the unsteady will
And hardens you against the chill
    Voice of a world of lies.
This amber medicine implants
Steadfastness in your blood; this grants
Immunity from greed and chance,
    And from all compromise.

This is the serum that can cure
Weak hearts; these pure, clear drops insure
You'll face what comes and can endure
    The test; you'll never falter.
This is the potion that preserves
You in a faith that never swerves;
This sets the pattern of your nerves
    Too firm for you to alter.

I set this spoon between your tight
Teeth, as I gave you your first bite;
This satisfies your appetite
    For other nourishment.
Take this on your tongue; this do
Remembering your mother who
So loved her Leader she stayed true
    When all the others went,

When every friend proved false, in the
Delirium of treachery
On every hand, when even He
    Had turned His face aside.
He shut himself in with His whore;
Then, though I screamed outside His door,
Said He'd not see me anymore.
    They both took cyanide.

Open wide, now, little bird;
I who sang you your first word
Soothe away every sound you've heard
    Except your Leader's voice.
Close your eyes, now; take your death.
Once we slapped you to take breath.
Vengeance is mine, the Lord God saith
    And cancels each last choice.

Once, my first words marked out your mind;
Just as our Leader's phrases bind
All hearts to Him, building a blind
    Loyalty through the nation,
We shape you into a pure form.
Trapped, our best soldiers tricked the storm,
The Reds: those last hours, they felt warm
    Who stood fast to their station.

You needn't fear what your life meant;
You won't curse how your hours were spent;
You'll grow like your own monument
    To all things sure and good,
Fixed like a frieze in high relief
Of granite figures that our Chief
Accepts into His true belief,
    His true blood-brotherhood.

You'll never bite the hand that fed you,
Won't turn away from those that bred you,
Comforted your nights and led you
    Into the thought of virtue;
You won't be turned from your own bed;
Won't turn into that thing you dread;
No new betrayal lies ahead;
    Now no one else can hurt you.

Hermann Göring,
Former Reichsmarschall

—30 April 1945

(Disowned by Hitler, arrested by S.S. troops, Göring does not know whether he will be executed or fall into American hands. In his castle at Mauterndorf—left him by his mother's lover—he stands, naked, before a full-length bedroom mirror.)

When I speak to you, you stand to attention.
Straighten that back up. Lift up your damn head.
You'd featherbed your life out on some pension?
Fat chance of that, Fat Man! You're here to die.
You can't haul that much pork up in the sky
And if you go down and you fry instead
You'll spit like bacon. You lost your nerve
To face the life you once had; why not try
Making your exit with some style, some verve?

Disowned and disinherited? Poor baby!
We'll make a man of you, you slab of blubber.
We'll teach you where your toes are, your spine—maybe
Work you back down to fighting weight again.
Go turn in your silk robes, your diamonds, then
Give back all the paintings, cash in your rubber
Medals for the tub. From those big loose dugs
You'll get no warm milk. Join the world of men
Where pain and death live. And check in your drugs.

You might just as well know just what you've done
Though that's not what they'll hang you for.
You took a fine officer's wife and son;
When you came to power you supplied
Facts that got your friend, Roehm, killed. Then you lied
About Blomberg and Fritsch. To start this war,
You threatened to bomb Prague; and your lies scared
Poor old Hacha who gasped, fell, almost died.
Speak up to your Chief, though—you never dared.

No; one more time, you let yourself be mastered
By someone you sucked up to—who used your blind
Faith, used your worst impulses, then the bastard
Took your honor. You bought your consequences.
Let Speer or Funk whimper and whine repentance
Merely to piss in front and crap behind
A few days more. You can't keep all *that* skin;
Keep some honor. You signed on for your sentence;
You're in so deep, there's no out left but in.

Your father lost the good name he'd once owned
By trying to fink out on his own past—
Your mother played whore; he'd ignored, condoned
That, years, to keep his soft life as a vassal
To Dr. Epenstein, lord of this castle
He left you. Well, nice guys finish last
And you're about to finish. Own your own
Decisions; own your men. And if some asshole
Stands to face you down, you stand alone.

*(Learning that Hitler's will names
Doenitz as successor, Himmler ponders
his alternatives. MM=104.)*

AN · EYE - PATCH · THATS · THE · ANSWER ·
BESIDES · ILL · SHAVE · MY · MOUSTACHE
CUT · MY · HAIR · ALL · WRONG · THERE · MY
DISGUISE · IS · COMPLETE · ILL · WEAR ·
EYEGLASSES · NOT · THIS · PINCE - NEZ ·

FALL · INTO · THE · MOBS · OF · REFUGEES
GOING · WEST · IVE · BECOME · HEINRICH
HITZINGER · WITH · THE · LEGITIMATE ·
IDENTITY · CARD · OF · A · SOLDIER · WE ·
JUST · SHOT · AS · A · DESERTER · STILL ·

KROSIG · SAYS · THE · ONLY · HONORABLE
LINE · IS · JUST · DRIVE · STRAIGHT · TO
MONTGOMERYS · H · Q · & · TELL · THEM · MY
NAME · IS · HEINRICH · HIMMLER · I · CAN
OFFER · MY · FORCES · SURRENDER · I · AM

PERSONALLY · RESPONSIBLE · WITHOUT
QUALIFICATION · FOR · ALL · S · S · ACTS
REALLY · NOW · WHY · NOT · JUST · SIMPLY
SHOOT · MYSELF · COULD · WE · GO · NORTH
TO · SCHLESWIG - HOLSTEIN · THEN · SET

UP · AN · S · S · GOVT · WE · MIGHT · OBTAIN
VERY · FAVORABLE · TERMS · FROM · THE ·
WEST · SO · THEN · AT · THE · VERY · WORST
YOUD · KEEP · OUT · OF · THE · HANDS · OF ·
ZHUKOV · AND · THE · RED · TROOPS · THE ·

AMERICANS · OBVIOUSLY · THEY · WOULD
BE · BEST · BUT · WE · HAVE · NO · JEWS · WE
CAN · TRADE · NO · PRISONERS · WE · MUST
DO · WHAT · WE · CAN · TO · CONVINCE · OUR
ENEMIES · THESE · ARE · SUBSTANTIAL ·

FORCES · BETTER · YET · WHY · CANT · WE ·
GO · TO · FLENSBURG · WITH · DOENITZ · &
HIS · CABINET · HITLERS · WILL · FLUNG
INTO · POWER · LINE · UP · OUR · CARS · & ·
JOIN · HIS · ENTOURAGE · WHOLL · DARE ·

KEEP · US · OUT · BESIDES · NOW · THEYRE
LIKE · ANY · GOVT · THEY · NEED · ARMED ·
MEN · TO · STAY · IN · POWER · SO · THEYLL
NEED · US · EVEN · TO · SURRENDER · ILL ·
OFFER · MY · SERVICES · AND · DEMAND · A

POST · SAY · HEAD · OF · POLICE · WE · CAN
QUASH · THIS · SO-CALLED · LAST · WILL
REALLY · HES · NOT · BEEN · HIMSELF · MY
STARS · STILL · SAY · I · MUST · SUCCEED
THE · CHIEF · ALTHOUGH · ITS · HARD · TO

UNDERSTAND · HOW · THAT · CAN · BE · SO ·
VERY · PUZZLING · STILL · FLENSBURGS
WHERE · YOUR · CHANCE · MAY · COME · OR ·
YOU · CAN · ALWAYS · BITE · INTO · THIS ·
ZINC · CAPSULE · & · WHAT · WHAT · WHAT ·

Dr. Joseph Goebbels

—1 May 1945, 1800 hours

> *(The day after Hitler's death, Goebbels
> and his wife climbed the steps into the
> garden where both committed suicide.)*

Say goodbye to the help, the ranks
Of Stalin-bait. Give too much thanks
To Naumann—Magda's lover: we
Thank him for *all* his loyalty.
Schwaegermann; Rach. After a while
Turn back to them with a sad smile:
We'll save them trouble—no one cares
Just now to carry us upstairs.

Turn away; check your manicure;
Pull on your gloves. Take time; make sure
The hat brim curves though the hat's straight.
Give her your arm. Let the fools wait;
They act like they've someplace to go.
Take the stairs, now. Self-control. Slow.
A slight limp; just enough to see,
Pass on, and infect history.

The rest is silence. Left like sperm
In a stranger's gut, waiting its term,
Each thought, each step lies; the roots spread.
They'll believe in us when we're dead.
When we took "Red Berlin" we found
We always worked best underground.
So; the vile body turns to spirit
That speaks soundlessly. They'll hear it.

If Birds Build
with Your Hair

A Phoebe's Nest

This green is the green of live moss;
This gray is the breast-feathers' down;
This tan, tough vine-roots;
This brown, dead needles of longleaf pine;

And this, this coppery fine filament
That glints like the light-weight wire
Boys wind off a motor core,
This is my own love's hair.

It's 7% and escrow;
It's Mary Jane and despair;
The ancient aunts say: headaches if
Birds build with your hair.

Near our hedgerow, in a nest snarled
Like a fright-wig, young hawks shriek;
Great red-tails sail our winds all day
While small birds peck at their heads.

But under our kitchen floorboards
Where live wires wind through the dark
Our crewcut phoebe plaited this nest
Like a jetset high pompadour.

Will the birds get dandruff?
Or pubic lice?
Will we go bald as an egg?

They'll knit a fine pucket
To warm up their brats;
You'll find out what'll ache.

This oriole's basket is woven white
Hair of our wolfhound, gone for years;
Our walls are rough plaster, laced with
The oxen's manes that worked this place.

Up under our roofpeak, birds slip
Through the roughcut cherry and beech;
Bare yards over the head of our bed
Strange bills squabble and screech.

It's Starlings stuck down the chimney;
It's where did you go? Nowhere.
It's peckerholes in the siding
And why did you park there?
It's swallows barnstorming the garage.
Things get in your hair.

Sometimes you find the young birds
Gone; other times they're dead;
Ones that stay faithfulest to their nest
Just somehow never got fed. Yet

Nerve ends circuit a memory;
Phone calls lattice the night;
That phoebe shuttled our cellardoor
All day every day of her life.

Some say better not get involved;
    Send Hallmark if you care;
Some say they've come a long way
    And haven't got much to spare;
Some say they're gonna have some fun;
    Too bad you don't dare;
Some say it just isn't fair;
    It stretches but it well might tear;
Get nylon or get wash-and-wear;
    They want their fair share.

Polish ciocias, toothless flirts
    Whose breasts dangle down to there,
Triple sea-hags say: headaches if
    Birds build with your hair.

Still, my lady's brushing-in sunlight
Near our silver maples where,
Like Christmas strings or bright beadwork
We loop loose strands of her hair.

Old Apple Trees

Like battered old millhands, they stand in the orchard—
Like drunk legionnaires, heaving themselves up,
Lurching to attention. Not one of them wobbles
The same way as another. Uniforms won't fit them—
All those cramps, humps, bulges. Here, a limb's gone;
There, rain and corruption have eaten the whole core.
They've all grown too tall, too thick, or too something.
Like men bent too long over desks, engines, benches,
Or bent under mailsacks, under loss.
They've seen too much history and bad weather, grown
Around rocks, into high winds, diseases, grown
Too long to be willful, too long to be changed.

Oh, I could replant, bulldoze the lot,
Get nursery stock, all the latest ornamentals,
Make the whole place look like a suburb,
Each limb sleek as a teeny bopper's—pink
To the very crotch—each trunk smoothed, ideal
As the fantasy life of an adman.
We might just own the Arboreal Muscle Beach:
Each tree disguised as its neighbor. Or each disguised
As if not its neighbor—each doing its own thing
Like executives' children.

At least I could prune,
At least I should trim the dead wood; fill holes
Where rain collects and decay starts. Well, I should;
I should. There's a red squirrel nests here someplace.
I live in the hope of hearing one saw-whet owl.
Then, too, they're right about Spring. Bees hum
Through these branches like lascivious intentions. The white
Petals drift down, sift across the ground; this air's so rich
No man should come here except on a working pass;
No man should leave here without going to confession.
All Fall, apples nearly crack the boughs;
They hang here red as candles in the
White oncoming snow.

Tonight we'll drive down to the bad part of town
To the New Hungarian Bar or the Klub Polski,
To the Old Hellas where we'll eat the new spring lamb;
Drink good *mavrodaphne*, say, at the Laikon Bar,
Send drinks to the dancers, those meatcutters and laborers
Who move in their native dances, the archaic forms.
Maybe we'll still find our old crone selling chestnuts,
Whose toothless gums can spit out fifteen languages,
Who turns, there, late at night, in the center of the floor,
Her ancient dry hips wheeling their slow, slow *tsamikos*;
We'll stomp under the tables, whistle, we'll all hiss
Till even the belly dancer leaves, disgraced.

We'll drive back, lushed and vacant, in the first dawn;
Out of the light gray mists may rise our flowering
Orchard, the rough trunks holding their formations
Like elders of Colonus, the old men of Thebes
Tossing their white hair, almost whispering,

Soon, each one of us will be taken
By dark powers under this ground
That drove us here, that warped us.
Not one of us got it his own way.
Nothing like any one of us
Will be seen again, forever.
Each of us held some noble shape in mind.
It seemed better that we kept alive.

Cherry Saplings

—for Russ

You turn your back on them no more
   Than for ten seconds—somebody's got to them.
Weed trees crop up, shadowing them under,
   Tent worms or aphids waste the leaves,
Rot leaches down from a torn branch,
   Woodrats gnaw them, girdle them around.
Take the whole Fall setting them in
   Sunlight, shaping, firming in their soil,
Come Springtime, find some Skidoo
   Snapped them clean off, back to the root.

When white men came to the continent
   First, they grew four feet through the trunk.
Try buying some new cherry, say,
   Six inches wide. Oh, you can find
The old boards still—whole table tops—
   The way you'll still see chestnut cupboards
Or find cross-grained elm chairs for some
   Years yet. We're good and done, though, with
Those broadest old trees, with the tallest.
   Cherries; these are merely the loveliest.

You'd think it was hard for them to take.
   They used it up in horse stalls, barn planks;
That curving tough grain went to roof in
   Dry lives, got buried in the walls
That fixed their hungers, their old wounds, their pride.
   That long-hardened heartwood with its clear
Rays quartering, spreading from the core,
   The ways they stained it—dried milk, dried blood,
Tobacco juice—until it gave way
   To the numbed image ruling their desires.

You'd think they thought it had grown too fine.
   They *never* thought of it. They had their dream.
The saplings stay, though, small stands of them,
   Or alone, there, under other trees,
The satiny red bark, the blown white flowers,
   Their thin trunks leaning outward, outward,
Feeling toward some memory of sun. It is
   Too late to cable them back upright,
Too late to cut down anything around.
   We have no right but to our own grounds.
What will we leave here still worth our hate?

Owls

—for Camille

Wait; the great horned owls
Calling from the wood's edge; listen.
There: the dark male, low
And booming, tremoring the whole valley.
There: the female, resolving, answering
High and clear, restoring silence.
The chilly woods draw in
Their breath, slow, waiting, and now both
Sound out together, close to harmony.

These are the year's worst nights.
Ice glazed on the top boughs,
Old snow deep on the ground,
Snow in the red-tailed hawks'
Nests they take for their own.
Nothing crosses the crusted ground.
No squirrels, no rabbits, the mice gone,
No crow has young yet they can steal.
These nights the iron air clangs
Like the gates of a cell block, blank
And black as the inside of your chest.

Now, the great owls take
The air, the male's calls take
Depth on and resonance, they take
A rough nest, take their mate
And, opening out long wings, take
Flight, unguided and apart, to caliper
The blind synapse their voices cross
Over the dead white fields,
The dead black woods, where they take
Soundings on nothing fast, take
Soundings on each other, each alone.

An Elm Tree

—in memory of Albert Herrick

The winter birds have come;
One of them knows my name:
    Chick-a-dee-dee-dee-dee-dee.
Now, a whole pack of them

Skinning past like hoods;
Up in the maples, hidden,
    One shuffles his deck of wings
And deals me a word, a word;

Then, like a struck spark, gone.
Yet, there's my sentence again
    From an oak branch overhead;
Another one, farther on

Jeers me behind the barn
Where the old path turns
    Past the smoldering mound
Where years of rubbish burn,

And out beyond to the grove
Of pine trees, chill as the grave,
    Where the sun's light never falls
But needles, steady as grief,

Sift up, muffling and soft,
The lower limbs crack off,
    And you sink halfway to the knee
In what shone green, aloft,

What will seep down and in
Before it sees light again.
        You *could* stop, but the bird
Says your name, then

You come out into the whole
Light of day on the hill
        Where, on the high cleared brow
Strongly arching still

Stands that blighted elm,
Rawboned, overwhelmed,
        Stripped like the old mad king
Of this vegetable realm.

This was your great-uncle's tree
That he watered every day—
        30 buckets and the spring
Half a mile away.

The leaves gone and the bark.
As if a man stood, stark,
        Till all had fallen away
But the nerves' field thrown on the dark

Woods behind his back.
A small boy, you came to the shack
        Where he lived alone on his land;
You felt ashamed and sick

At the dark, heavy stain
On your thin wrist all day
    After he shook your hand.
May that not wash away.

Coming Down from the Acropolis

We bent our backs, the two of us, climbing
    That stony yellow hillside, together, to the
Cleared high ground. Already we had climbed
    Castle hills, climbed *schloss, grad* and *var,*
The Kehlstein above Berchtesgaden, Rakoczi's Bastion,
    Traced bullet-pocked walls, the charred siege-gates,
The low, sodden death-camps, gray with horror.
    Here we had arrived at the ancient, sacred ring
Where the West turned from its wars to raise
    White marble, ordinate and clean as
Nursery furniture. Here, every line, every measure
    Led the eye to its security, to its calm.
And this had nourished the thinking of all Europe.
    Of course the temple roof is gone; its stone images
Stripped. The altar ground lies open to rain; it cannot
    Be visited. At random, some unbearing columns stand
Like an elm grove, blighted. Cigar butts underfoot,
    Used Kodak wrappers, orange peels, old drums of marble
Each-which-way like a Scrabble set somebody dropped.
    Below us, the new Athens smoked and clattered, living
Off this dead trunk to support its tourists' light shows,
    Its miles of huckster shops, its bouzoukee joints.
In those public squares where excellence defined itself,
    Impotent crowds brag of their freedom, argue policy;
They cringe under a tyrant-clown propped up in place
    By our own CIA. How quick, how easy the decline,
How quickly they forgot, hot for a different vision.
    They chose and, choosing, took the thief, the liar,
And felt at home with that. Phidias, whose hand carved it,
    Died in their jails. They turned from Pericles, turned
On their own; Greek fought with Greek or sold
    His skill to strangers, to his enemies. And all that time,
We both knew that our own state would choose the same.
    When we came back down to the foot, we sat, together,
On a fallen stone. We said some few, some ugly words
    Then turned our backs; each took his separate way.

Setting Out

Staying here, we turn inflexible,
Stiffening under laws that drive
Sap through the tight stems,
Roots to break down rock;
Relentless as the fall
Of rhymes in a folk ballad.
You are called toward someone free
To come or go as the wind's whim,
Casual as the air whistles,
Trembling all that stands with
Mortal touch, while your hand
Slips through every which way.

Here, we find ourselves unstable
As our fields: crops, cloud-
shadows wash across us;
The various weed-flowers fade
To flat snow; dogs tear
Our deer; streams flow again . . .
You are drawn to someone constant
As a room where the costly wallpaper
Blooms in half-light,
Where at last somebody dearly
Loved is always almost
Ready to appear.

We know we turn exacting,
Monotonous as the hours
Wheel, as the seasons
Wheel, as the arrogant
Stars turn wheeling on their
Cold, determined track.
Go, then, find someone tender
As a child's eyelid closing
In his first sleep, shy
As the warm scent we all seek,
That mild and absent voice
Numbing the sense away.

Perhaps, who knows, in so much
Searching you may not be lost;
Paths you take may take you
Into comfort past our thought;
It may be the finding
Won't enervate your grasp.
You can find us here, still
Going about our rounds,
Fingering out the beat
Of old songs, fixed on ways
Worn out as a star chart,
Unimaginably far.

Seasoning Barn

—for Roy Sheldon

Here in the darkness of these dry, bird-sounding lofts,
The rough thick boards, sawn and stacked up, lie
Under the dusts that sift down over them
     fifteen, maybe twenty years.
It's echoing here, as cool as a catacombs and,
Truly, they are one company of the elect—
Their generation gone into firewood and to rot.
The tides that have broken over them, coursed through them,
Which they were made to carry, gradually go out;
They keep some movement still, a reverberation:
They shrink a little, draw into themselves
Till they turn harder, more virtual, so lighter,
Till they reach their balance with the air.

They are like mirrors reflecting on themselves all night,
As if we thought about our dreams until our dreams
Had dreams about their dreaming.

They lie here, though, as dull as gray old ledgerbooks
Someone's forgotten in a back angle of some attic,
Dull as old *Life*s, bound, laid up in a library,
Dull as mud samplings, as another language.
     Yet, to the right eye, closed
On the accounts, extortions, strategies lives are built by:
Here are the crimes and follies, the beliefs and lies;
Here, the old injuries, the wretchedness when young, forced growth,
Diseases, aims and accidents, the reachings out that
Failed and were buried, live, in the living knots;
Here, in the dark, these change toward changelessness.

Until the right eye and the right hand comes,
The old man with his cat,
                         and lifts them out of here.
He is not looking for the clear, straight grain—
The single consistent color. Leave that to the factories;
It might as well be stained. He's searching
For the sworls and twists, for those deep flaws that mean
Character in the finished work—pithmarks and ingrowings.
He cuts down through the surface; his radio fills the barn with,
Strangely, Brahms. His sure abrasive touch
Will open out, irregular as high-tide marks, telling
As a thumbprint, the topographies of growth: here
Are the open rings of Springtime and the solid summers;
Here the light sapwood, here the heavier, dark heartwood;
Under his hand the darkest knots take on a deeper burnish.
And in some few he can hope to find that luminous figuring
Of the rays that stored and carried sustenance out to the growing edge,
Inward to the core.
                         When he has shaped and planed these, he will sand
And rub by hand, building a finish, hour after hour.

And the old man sits down, rubbing the cat's ears,
Or hikes up his suspenders and walks home.

A
Locked House

Silver Poplars

That winking, glimmering like the wings
    of starlings in their dark flock, wheeling
        into the last light, into the light breeze;
that shivering like lake ripples, like sequins
    on a black lace veil that half reveals
        some face which, loveliest, lies beneath;
that soft shade we once sat to read in
    afternoons, and on then, on through evenings
        one with that tremulous, steady breath;
that giving, true to each slightest wind's
    least impulse, caught where the leaf
        yields up its pale down, underneath:—

done for, gone, down in one night's storm
    to close out twenty-five years' growing,
        gone, that we had meant to stand
watch at our dooryard, to stand firm
    through even its own changing—green,
        yellow, bare, then green again—to stand
for us. For what stands. What rainfall then turned
    stiff that bitter midnight, all unseen,
        glazed and enameled every stunned
numb leaf and twig? By dawn, the whole frame burned
    rigid with enchantment. Each sinew strained,
        shuddering, determined, but the charged tree bent
and shattered. In full daylight, one, torn
    out like a mind from its own ground
        of understanding, sprawled its full length;
split down the main trunk, skewed like some deformed
    drunk lurching through the park, the second
        wears out a sort of half-life to its end.

Not much you can do with it; tends to splinter
  on you, check or twist, suppose it's been left
    years to season. Chainsaw; stack the leavings
against chill mornings, what with winter
  coming on. For all that figured grain, too soft
    to last long; too soft for much real heating.

Mutability

It was all different; that, at least, seemed sure.
We still agreed—but only that she'd changed.
Some things that you still loved might still endure.

You woke in your own, big, dove-tailed bed, secure
And warm—but the whole room felt rearranged.
It was all different; that, at least, seemed sure.

The lamp stood four-square—like your furniture;
The air'd gone tinged, though, or the light deranged.
Some things that you still loved might still endure

Outside. Your fields stretched, a parched upland moor
Where shadows paired and split, where lean shapes ranged.
It was all different; that, at least, seemed sure

And that, from here on in, you could count on fewer
Second chances. Some rules might be arranged;
Some things that you still loved might still endure,

Though some old friends would close, soon, for the pure
Joy of the kill—no prisoners exchanged.
It was all different; that, at least, seemed sure.

Maybe the injuries weren't past all cure.
No luck lasts; yours might not, too long, stay estranged;
Some things that you still loved might still endure.
It was all different; that, at least, seemed sure.

The Last Time

Three years ago, one last time, you forgot
Yourself and let your hand, all gentleness,
Move to my hair, then slip down to caress
My cheek, my neck. My breath failed me; I thought

It might all come back yet, believed you might
Turn back. You turned, then, once more to your own
Talk with that tall young man in whom you'd shown,
In front of all our friends, such clear delight

All afternoon. You recalled, then, the long
Love you had held for me was changed. You threw
Both arms around him, kissed him, and then you
Said you were ready and we went along.

A Locked House

As we drove back, crossing the hill,
The house still
Hidden in the trees, I always thought—
A fool's fear—that it might have caught
Fire, someone could have broken in.
As if things must have been
Too good here. Still, we always found
It locked tight, safe and sound.

I mentioned that, once, as a joke;
No doubt we spoke
Of the absurdity
To fear some dour god's jealousy
Of our good fortune. From the farm
Next door, our neighbors saw no harm
Came to the things we cared for here.
What did we have to fear?

Maybe I should have thought: all
Such things rot, fall—
Barns, houses, furniture.
We two are stronger than we were
Apart; we've grown
Together. Everything we own
Can burn; we know what counts—some such
Idea. We said as much.

We'd watched friends driven to betray;
Felt that love drained away
Some self they need.
We'd said love, like a growth, can feed
On hate we turn in and disguise;
We warned ourselves. That you might despise
Me—hate all we both loved best—
None of us ever guessed.

The house still stands, locked, as it stood
Untouched a good
Two years after you went.
Some things passed in the settlement;
Some things slipped away. Enough's left
That I come back sometimes. The theft
And vandalism were our own.
Maybe we should have known.

A Seashell

Say that inside this shell, some live
Thing hungered, trembled to survive,
Mated, died. Lift this to your ear
The way the young, on tape decks, hear
What to become, or on the phone,
The old evoke a dial tone
To what they had. Your blood will pound
Down those bare chambers, then resound
Your own ear's caverns as a ground

Bass swells, the depths of some salt tide
Still tuned to our salt blood. Outside,
The woods, nights, still ring back each word.
Our young owl, though, that always heard
My hoot, then veered down through the dark,
Our fox that barked back when we'd bark,
Won't answer, though. Small loss, now, when
Friends ask that I not call again.
Our pulse homed in on each other's, then.

Last night, I heard your voice—caught on
Streets we once taped in Isfahan;
Then, in a mosque near Joppa, blent
With hushed devotions and lament.
Now, put the shell back down, at rest
Near this brain coral, this wren's nest,
These photographs that will stand here
On their shelf in the silent, dear,
Locked, empty house another year.

Old Jewelry

This Gypsy bodice of old coins
   From seven countries, woven fast
So that a silver braidwork joins
   The years and places their tribe passed;

This crown-shaped belt, cast in Soufli—
   Jeweled, enameling on silver-gilt—
A trothplight, then that surety
   On which a family would be built;

This Roman fibula, intact
   From the fourth century though bent;
This Berber fibula, once blacked
   With layers of thick tar to prevent

Theft but that, scoured and polished, shone
   As luminous as it ever was;
This lapis, Persian, the unfading stone
   Gold-flecked and implicate with flaws;

Brass arm bands, rings, pins, bracelets, earrings—
   Something from nearly every place
We'd been. Once more to see these dear things
   Laid out for buyers in a glass showcase.

I'd known them, each one—weighed in hand,
   Rubbed, bargained, and then with my love,
Pinned each one on for her, to stand
   In fickle times for emblems of

What lasts—just as they must have once
   For someone long dead. Love that dies
Can still be wrung out for quick funds;
   No doubt someone would pay the price.

A Valediction

Since his sharp sight has taught you
To think your own thoughts and to see
What cramped horizons my arms brought you,
    Turn then and go free,

    Unlimited, your own
Forever. Let your vision be
In your own interests; you've outgrown
    All need for tyranny.

May his clear views save you
From those shrewd, undermining powers
That hold you close just to enslave you
    In some such love as ours.

May this new love leave you
Your own being; may your bright rebirth
Prove treacherous, change then and deceive you
    Never on this earth.

Now that you've seen how mindless
Our long ties were, I pray you never
Find, all your life through, such a blindness
    As we two shared together.

My dark design's exposed
Since his tongue opened up your eyelids;
May no one ever lip them closed
    So cunningly as I did.

D. D. Byrde
Callyng
Jennie Wrenn

—for K. T. Browne

Deare wee Browne Byrdie, dare wee too
    Hazzerd an aire togeather?—
A perkie Maytime chickke like yew,
    Me in my frosstie feather?

I bee noe Admirabl Byrde
    Yet sailed the Polar Blizzerd,
Frose all my tose upp and incurred
    Muche miserie in my gizzerd.

Above those icie glares these goggels
    Dimmed thru winters fiftie;
Now mine eye dazzels, my sight boggels:—
    Yea, Byrdie, thou art niftie!

Thy spruce bright eye and bubbelie tonge
    Like gin upspike my tonick,
Surcharginge my Septembre Songe
    To pulse fowrth supersonick.

Thy pert bobtaile and sundrie pritties
    Brim this olde craw to flowe
With Springtime's light, lassivius ditties
    That state: "Byrdes mate, you noe?"

Com sing beside me; fetche thy bottel
    Of joye's best anti-freese;
Torch upp my pipes; pull out my throttel;
    Sparke these darke synapsees.

These shivverie drye bones yearn to test
   A cosy brest of browne
Where deep limb-tangel snugs thy nest
   And feathers are alle downe.

Ginnie Jen, Ginnie Jen, come juice upp these joints;
   De-ice these rime-tipt wings;
Race my pace-maker, gapp my points—
   We'll try som cuppel sings.

O ginnie Jennie, June's long passt
   For stiff olde joints like these;
Still, olde stiff joints could learn to lasst
   Wert thou a chickke-a-dee's.

What iff lean, hawkish sharp-shinnd Age
   Fixxeth me in his sights?
This olde pump's rattelinge its cage
   Too try yewnited flights.

Tho I, in my Lone Rangyr Masque,
   Soon soloe into som sunsett,
Dare famelie, frends or strangyrs ask
   Uss not to duet oncet?

Since soleful witt must needs bee briefe,
   Let me noe more waxxe wordie:
If *yew* don't mind, I'd just as lief;
   Ten-fowr to thee, Browne Byrdie.

Kinder Capers

The poems in Kinder Capers
are related to paintings
by DeLoss McGraw

Through the Nursery Window

—*for Dylan Taylor McGraw*

There, there, sir. You have every cause
For tears; which of us blames your grief?
Knowing what high estate you've lost,
What powers, what opulence you leave,

That you must give up absolute
Dominion, sole rule of a spot
Where all desires, even your slightest
Wish before that wish was thought

Was satisfied, where you commanded
All breathing things in pashadom
And empiry safe and sure, a land
Which was, in brief, the paradigm

Of every human heart's least earthly
Paradise—how this could be torn
By gross upheaval against your worthy
Person and sweet governance, could turn

You out of doors, roughly . . . dear sir,
To banish you, unknown, abandoned
By followers, washed up on this shore
With no funds, not a leg to stand on,

Helpless to feed and clothe your poor
Small self—truly, it would be best
To think of other matters. Spare
Your eyes, your breath. Try; try to rest.

Have patience with your temporary
Poor berth; we've filled out all your papers
To leave this general dormitory
For what suits with your rank and nature.

A lovely woman, a brilliant man
Will shelter and guard you, help you learn
Your new name, learn our tongue and manners,
Learn that a living can be earned.

If this is not, dear sir, Illyria,
It has its range of choices, freedom
To follow whatever calls might lure you
Into the bounties rude coasts can afford.

You may find, soon, that old life bland,
Short on challenge, too confining for you.
We need your wits, charm, ambition, and
The wilderness lies all before you . . .

True, things may never seem so lovely
From now on. Still, a sort of life
Exists; things can get somewhat lively
Picnicking with our half a loaf

And chipped wine jug. Some have felt glad
They'd set foot over this dark sill.
May your new family have a good
Baby; you have a good exile.

Part I
The Death
of
Cock Robin

The Charges Against Cock Robin

Speaker: His Honor James T. "Just
call me Jim" Crowe.

Chorus: Titmouse and Dormouse, Eagle
and Seagull, Cuckoo and Water Shrew.

It is charged he's been known to warble
        (Deplorable!)
An aria, a love song, or recitatif
        (Good Grief!)
When he goes walking, long after curfew
        (God preserve you!)
Waking both town and country.
        (What effrontery!)

We find it far more injurious
        (We're just furious!)
That he sings beyond other birds' range
        (He's strange!)
Though they practice and pay the best teachers
        (Poor creatures!)
While his tunes baffle us and defeat us.
        (Elitist!)

Moreover, he dresses in a fashion
        (Far too dashing!)
Neither generic nor respectable—
        (Get expectable!)
All sorts of bright shreds and patches
        (Nothing matches!)
That make no more sense than cuneiform.
        (Get a uniform!)

If one wishes to sound operatic
                    (We're emphatic!)
Or to break forth with a cantata
                    (All birds oughta)
Always be careful to bring along
                    (Like a singalong)
Fitting clothes and a high-sounding moral.
                    (Get oral; get choral; wax floral!)

He is urged by us birds of one stripe
                    (Be our type!)
And enjoined by us cats of one color
                    (Get duller!)
Be a horse of one congruous feather.
                    (All together.)
Cease these lyrics of lust, rum and riot
                    (Keep it quiet!)
And incitements to profligate violence.
                    (Silence!)

W. D., Don't Fear That Animal

My hat leaps up when I behold
   A rhino in the sky;
When crocodiles upon the wing
Perch on my windowsill to sing
All my loose ends turn blue and cold;
      I don't know why.

My knuckles whiten should I hark
   Some lonely python's cry;
Should a migrating wedge of moose
Honk, it can shake my molars loose—
Or when, at heaven's gate, the shark
      Doth pine and sigh.

My socks may slide off at the sight
   Of giant squids on high
Or baby scorpions bubbling up
Inside my morning coffee cup—
Somehow, it spoils my appetite;
      My throat gets dry.

At dawn, I lift my gaze in air
   Cock Robin to espy
And mark instead some bright-eyed grizzly;
The hairs back of my neck turn bristly.
That's foolish since it's clear that they're
      More scared than I.

Such innocent creatures mean no harm;
    They wouldn't hurt a fly.
Still, when I find myself between a
Playful assembly of hyena,
I can't help feeling some alarm;
        I've got to try.

W. D. Lifts Ten Times
the Weight of
His Own Body

1.

These Russian heavies are all wrong
On force and form. No doubt they're strong
But if you turn into a hulk
Of mass and muscle, your own bulk
Can drop you into a deep oxtrap:
You lift yourself by your own jockstrap
Besides those weights you jerk and press;
So it's essential to weigh less,
Embodying uplift and *ballon*.
The way these Russians put weight on
You'd think it's going out of style. It's gone.

One lad I knew hefted a heifer
Daily; it grew light as a zephyr
Even when swollen to its full
Beefy bloatitude as a bull.
Myself, I uphold every day
The self-same load, but meanwhile weigh
Less than I did the day before.
Like ants, I now tote ten times more
Than my own tonnage. At the gym
I pare myself down, airier, slim,
Till I become a 98-
Pound Charles, at last, of underweight.
An auto-hoist, combating gravity,
I rise up in high spirits and levity,
Unbending my irreverent knee
To overcome brute force and mightiness;
Getting things off the ground takes flightiness.

2.

Snodgrass's Second Theorem states: You're
Stronger when bending to things' nature.
Don't lift; release things toward the skies—
Release what's meant, or means, to rise.
Raise jackstraws, piles of pickup sticks,
Spokes, pikes and pickets, spikes, toothpicks;
Raise kite sticks, stalks, struts, Roman candles,
Rays of bright sunlight, hafts, helves, handles;
Raise vaulters' poles, Olympic javelin
Shafts, sword strokes, streaks of starlight traveling
Through black wastes; raise up jet trails, tracers;
Raise fish rods, bike spokes, lances, lasers.
Be one with all things light and luminous
Like a Zen sage or some old Humanist
Whose drive to transport and to heighten meant
Shouldering a general Enlightenment.
Now, like a Chinese waiter, scoop
This universal mare's nest soup
To shoulder level, all the while
A fat moon peering through the pile
And cosmic tangle has to smile
To see Cock Robin, calm, at rest
And sleeping sound in that vast nest
Or twiggy burden, borne along
The steady airstream on a strong
Dream's wingbeat or on springs of song.

W. D. Is Concerned About the Character Assassination of Cock Robin

Yo no quiero verla;
Yo no lo se.

Come, Rosie Angel, clasp
    Over each eye, each ear,
Your gauze-soft hands that grasp
    What not to see or hear.

        Don't care to,
        Won't dare to,
        Can't bear to
           See.

Should the secret inspectors
    Knock once at your locked door,
Not even bill collectors
    Know your name any more.

        Don't choose to,
        Refuse to,
        No use to
           Hear.

As your stock falls, old friends
    Fall off. Fall into danger—
If you survive depends
    On some total stranger.

Past all thought;
Best forgot.
Surely not
Here.

Small wonder dear friends turn
Acrimonious and cruel
When Love's most fierce fires burn
Denatured hate for fuel.

Never more,
Neither nor,
Not friend or
Foe.

All you once knew goes strange.
Some you've known all their lives
Outside your window range,
Tongues flashing slick as knives

Numb, deaf, blind;
May we find
No man's mind
So.

Where Cock Robin's once-loved name
Sank like fat in the sands
And his good neighbors came
Licking their snouts and hands.

I'd deceive
All who'd grieve.
Come; believe
Me.

A face, now, fixed with wide
Open eyes, constantly
Loitering near outside,
Keeps close watch over me.

No, never;
Nerves, sever;
Don't ever
Know.

Yo no quiero verla;
Yo no lo se.

Lullaby:
The Comforting of Cock Robin

Smooth quill and bristle down;
Soothe day's shrill whistle down;
Bestow the head
To its own bed
Of soft moss and thistledown.

May the insatiable powers,
The vast cravings of the dark,
Spend their forces and their hours
Each on each, or miss their mark;

May the raccoon and the agile
Long-tailed, long-toothed squirrel pass,
Find the fox and miss the fragile
Clutch of eggs in the long grass.

May the weasel, the lithe snake,
May the housecat on the prowl,
Creeping up the limbs all night,
Meet and satisfy the owl.

Let the shivering eyelid close,
The down-surrounded egg, turn in
On the steady urge that grows
What might be from what has been

Till beneath the illusory lamps,
Burned out, the hankering moth miller
Sprawls, and toward fresh new green leaves tramps
The lockstep, workday caterpillar

While, fresh, the sprinkler on the lawn
    Lures the young, nutritious worm
To loll and sunbathe in the dawn,
    Plump, seductive, pink and firm.

Then shall your well-supported song,
    Drafting the full breath's thermal currents,
Carry the mastered woodlands, strong
    With portamento, with endurance.

        Smooth quill and bristle down;
        Soothe day's shrill whistle down;
          Bestow the head
          To its own bed
        Of soft moss and thistledown.

W. D. Tries to
Warn Cock Robin

The Brutish are coming; the Brutish;
The Rude-Coats with snares and bum-drumming!
    The Skittish and Prudish
    The Brattish and Crude
    Who'll check on your morals
    And find your song's lewd
Then strip off the bay leaves and laurels
That garnished your brows and your food,
All tongues and all tastebuds benumbing.
    They'll dull all your senses
    Then lull your defenses
And rule you through blue-nosed and tasteless pretenses;
    The Brutish!

The Ruffians are coming; the Ruffians!
Those rowdies with mandolins strumming!
    They'll stomp out your stuffings
    And all you've been taught;
    Pan-Slobs from Vulgaria
    Will come; if you're caught
Knowing more than your own name, they'll bury you.
Inter your own brain, so they'll not
Take more than your watch and your plumbing.
    Those red-necked invaders,
    Those radical raiders
Who'll root out free thinkers, free lovers, free traders!
    The Ruffians!

The Merkans are coming; the Merkans!
Those jingoes whose jingles keep gumming
      Your intimate workings
      With terms periphrastic;
      The fare that they offer
      Will ruin your gastric
Intestinal tract; then they'll cover
Your country with asphalt and plastic
To hide what keeps oozing and scumming.
      They'll plug up your juices,
      Slipcover your sluices,
Then turn your equipment to mercantile uses,
      The Merkans!

The Krishans are coming; the Krishans!
Hear the chants, psalms and hymns they keep humming!
      They'll offer you visions
      Of undying blisses
      With premises, promises,
      And crucifixes
To prop up all Questioning Thomases.
They'll double criss-cross you with kisses
And blessings. With grim mimes and mumming,
      The hairy one omming,
      The balded ones psalming,
      With rituals and riddles
      And charity victuals,
You'll jump into hellfire to get off their griddle;
      The Krishans!

The Youmans are coming; the Youmans!
Hear the backslapping rascals, the chumming
      Of Masculs and Woomans
      Who built up this Babel
      Of Atoms and Evils
      And hope that they're able
To raise further cain and upheavals.
That Garden foreclosed in the fable
Foretold how this world's going slumming:
      In cold greed, the cowards
      Still split and unite
      For unneeded powers,
      While backbiting spite
      Pulls down all their towers;
      With air, sea and soil
      And their own minds to spoil
And spin their bright cosmos to unending night;
      The Youmans!

W. D. Meets Mr. Evil while Removing the Record of Bartok and Replacing It with a Recent Recording by the Everly Brothers in Order to Create a Mood Conducive to Searching for Cock Robin

So; caught you in, my fine young fellow?
Thought I'd just drop past to say Hello,
Dish out some hot poop—how to find
The outlawed Redbreast on your mind:
His Cockiness whose Robinhood
Echoes the Forest of Sure Would.

I know *you*, though. Just call me Mystery
Bill, B.S., M.S. in doctored History,
Onetime Sheriff of Nothing Am,
Ambassador of Havasham,
Last Past Master of Hoke Lodge,
High Priest and Medium for Mirage.

First off, we've got to change the record—
Such grim sounds evidence a checkered
Past—then concoct an atmosphere full
Of hopeful tunes, loving and cheerful.
Dump these sour tones, this cleverly infernal
Dissonance; we'll choir forth an Everly eternal

Psalm of unchanging Brotherhood,
Fake chords real folks would like real good,
Cut platters of pattering platitudes
To impart the politic, pat attitudes
Taught by our founder, Dr. Garbles,
Who struck dumb multitudes with marbles

Held in mouthfuls of popular melody.
Or better still, this high fidelity
Digital of an eighteen minute
Gap: you'll feel, each time you spin it,
Pure as a Quaker, freed from violence
And expletives by blissful silence.

To lure down this bird you desire
We'll mute our loot, moot every liar,
Ban all Anacreonisms or Sapphics
Then chart this on our phoni-Graphics,
Banish gloom, gravity and art talk.
Besides, we'll lie about the Bartok.

W. D. Attempts
to Save Cock Robin

no sir i would not like to sell
this bird for soup yes sonnie i have heard
the polish joke and yes i know
the bird says get this joker
off my ass and indeed professor i have
seen that rembrandt with the small dog
shitting in the foreground so if you
could just inform me señor who
might own this bird or where it lives
or merely point me toward a
doctor and no fraulein kindly not
to a psychiatrist the bird
is real and heavy and the blood
gets down my neck mon capitaine but no
i am not familiar with the
napoleonic code so would you
please remove those handcuffs and
believe me no i do not have
a songbird license since quamlibet i
shot not this bird is there a
real need you behind the mask there
to lock me in this cage you see
WELL
i was practicing for
oberammergau and in this country
wood is too expensive for a cross

Coroner's Inquest

Who killed Cock Robin?
Don't you blyme me, says the sparrow;
I gone strictly straight-and-narrow,
Reformed, true-blue, a real straight arrow.
I never done that slob in.

Who saw him die?
Not I, certainly, says the fly;
My dear, this polyhedral eye
Can only make things out nearby.
I mind my own bee's wax; that's my
Alibi.

Who'll wash the body?
We know too well, says the raccoon,
He sang low songs, played the buffoon
In many a road house or saloon
From bawdy midnight to high noon.
It's only fitting that so soon
He's left lowdown and cruddy.

Who'll weave his shroud?
Our local folkarts, says the spider,
Are unbecoming an outsider
Or untraditional fore-slider
Who's rejected every guide or
Guideline, led by spiritual pride or
Sensual passion through a wider
World than we're allowed.

Who'll dig his grave?
I'm committed, says the mole,
To exploring my own hole
Liberated from control
Of any social, prefixed role;
I keep my deep molehood whole
Seeking my true self and soul.
My blind eye's fixed on this goal;
Go find a cave.

Who'll bear his casket?
Count me out there, says the ant.
I'm too small; I simply can't.
With my legion friends, I grant
We might, yet we're all adamant
That unless he should recant
Each lewd song and surreal chant
With their sly, anarchic slant,
Even if we could we shan't
So don't ask it.

Who'll say the last words?
Of course I'd like to, says the parrot;
I'm aware that all his merit
Was so rare we can't compare it,
Yet my grief and great despair at
This sad loss, if I should share it,
Is so vast, I couldn't bear it.
Then besides, my friends don't care at
All for anyone who'd dare it.
Those that sing strange songs inherit
Faint praise—few and fast words.

All the beasts of earth and air
　　Fell a-weaselin' and a-bobbin'
When they heard of the death
　　Of poor Cock Robin.

Call for Clues

Okay, you leaves up there, come clean;
Your turn to sing out: whattaya seen?
You can't just perch there high and mighty
Whispering, rubbing your palms politely.
Speak up; someday you gotta tumble
Down in the dirt, red-faced and humble
Just like him. Now, who done this bird?
Whattaya seen and whattaya heard?

Cough it up, clouds; you're on the hook.
Don't give me no vague, wandering look.
Maybe you're short on shape and "It-ness";
We know damn well you was a witness.
You took in loads; you been aroun';
It weighs on you; it's a bringdown
Holding back. Spill it all, posthaste:
Who brung that bird out here to waste?

Okay, you stars, you sun and moon,
Pipe up; we're here to cop your tune.
You gone past here, so come acrost.
You gonna let his tunes get lost,
Buried in self-important sounds
Or dead air, then just go your rounds?
Ain't no tight-lipped, black hat can frighten us.
You high-flown, radiant types, enlighten us.

Listen, you hunks of sky, blank spaces
Absent-minded above our faces,
Between all stars, all small-time particles:
Man, beast, bird, tree, all living articles
That slump down groundward, dead and rotten,
Fly off in you and get forgotten.
Save something wunst. Get this thing solved.
Vast tracts of nothing, get involved!

W. D. Sits in Kafka's Chair
and Is Interrogated Concerning
the Assumed Death of Cock Robin

Now "W"—we'll call you "W,"
    Okay? We like the friendly touch.
Just a few questions that won't trouble you
    For long; this won't hurt much.

First: name, age, sex, race, genus,
    Specific gravity and species;
Hat size, color of hair and penis;
    Texture and frequency of feces?

Republican? No? Then a Baptist.
    If not, why not? If so, explain
Why you switched sides. Did your last Pap test
    Turn pink or blue? Are you insane?

When did you halt, cease or desist
    Beating your wife? Was she friends
With this Cock Robin long? Please list
    Payments from foreign governments.

Have you changed sperm count or IQ
    Within six months? Signed a confession?
Why are we holding you? If you
    Don't know, then why ask you this question?

A simple yes or no is all
    We want; the truth always shines through.
Thank you. Please wait out in the hall
    Until somebody comes for you.

W. D. Creates
a Device for Escaping

After one first green step ahead,
I brake down on this foot of red;
        A stop foot, then a go foot.

One arm, one leg in my own spokes,
A balance wheel of counterstrokes,
        A to foot, then a fro foot.

These blood-red hands before my face,
Carrots that keep me at my pace,
        A fast foot, then a slow foot,

As a pit pony cranks a winch,
Ixion axles, inch by inch,
        A start foot, then a whoa foot,

Beneath the circling stars and seasons,
Time's roulette game of rhymes and reasons,
        A con foot, then a pro foot,

Plodding, wing-burdened like a pack,
This dead-weight Robin on my back,
        A heel foot, then a toe foot.

He wears my stripes, he rides my wheel;
How shall my galls and blisters heal?—
        A high foot, then a low foot—

And where do ten-ton Robins sleep?
On my back still while I still creep,
            A quid foot, then a quo foot.

I could cut loose, leaving him bound
To ride this giddy Fun-Go-Round,
            A joy foot, then a woe foot,

Or turn weak like old Sisyface,
Letting him roll back to the base;
            A yes foot, then a no foot.

Disguised as Cock Robin,
W. D. Escapes

Come, Rosie Angel, faced with blues,
   Join hands and we'll be piped together
      Pilots of our own quarter, decked
In multiplicity's fast hues—
   This Joseph's cloak that many a feather
      Weaves—in fact, a factory reject

That is becoming without seems.
   Fortuna's game wheel be our helm;
      We'll shoot the jazzy straits of I-Am,
Flee all Utopia's bonded schemes
   Of ideal bondage for a live realm
      Where I'll lush up my lute like Khayyam

While you beside me, blushing warm,
   Sing out like Saki. At this wheel
      We'll steer, veer, chart what course we shipped,
Skipped, slipped out, then rode out the storm
   Reeling our catch of all that *is* real
      Out of this land of Gyp and Be Gypped.

Assuming Fine Feathers,
W. D. Takes Flight

Over these cheekbones,
   Streaked thick with bristle,
Draw down the soft down
   Sleek as a whistle.
     See feedle, seedle, tweedle tree.

My slimy nostrils,
   My slithery lips
Turn to a beak, blunt
   As dry facts or tinsnips.
     Homo nonsapiens conturbat me.

These split lids fit
   My eye like a filter;
The dim world clicks
   To a new green kilter.
     Earclay, eanseclay ymay ightsay.

Scapular, spellbound,
   These feathers drape
My shoulderblades
   Like an opera cape
     Cheggange meggee; freggee meggee.

Or a Sioux priest's vestments;
   Dare to assume
The adept's full mantle
   And the long tail-plume.
     Sing-a-ling, wing-wary-way.

Through clouds of unknowing
   I veer and sail;
Below, men's heads
   And dogs' heads wail—
     In nubibus, ignotum per ignotius—

Hot on my track still,
   But I tricked 'em;
Now who's your criminal;
   Where's your victim?
     Dee-flee-a-beadle-tweedle-free!

W. D. Disguised as Cock Robin and Hidden Deep in Crimson

They'll never find me hidden
So close to them, inside
Switched-on electric wires
Or nerve ends, in forbidden
Urges, rage, lust, pride,
Sweet murderous desires,
The medulla of old fires.

I go cloaked in the charged rag
That matadors must wave
To keep them out of sight;
Protected by the flag
They run up in the brave
Country of Dynamite;
I lurk in the Geistzeit.

I ride the pulse that swells
Lips, nails, all feverish parts;
I wear the blushing scarlet
Alphabet that spells
The blazing braille of hearts,
The shorted shorts of the harlot,
Virgin, housewife, starlet.

I doppelgang some grander
Land that schizophrenics
Colonize from earth,
One with the salamander,
With that flaming phoenix
Or lodgepole pine whose clenched cones need
The forest fire to cast their seed.

Auction

For the gay tailfeathers, say, what'll you pay?—
Red, blue and purple plumes—a bouquet
Of heather-spume, or a lit fountain's spray. Hey!
Shave a fine penpoint, whisk dust away
Or trim sharp the virginals' quills when you play.

Who'll buy an eye—aye, buy an eye!
This ringset onyx jet, black tack for your tie
Or oldtimer's photocell, spy in the sky,
Laserbeam click-ticking off who's slipped by
Or to glow soft by the cribside till dawntide draws nigh.

What am I bid for this swift wing?—
A deft wing, an arched-out lifting thing
To nail fast on your hallwalls or set fling
The soul's boomerang, the young shepherd's sling
That brings huge despair down, crowns the new king.

How much for the bones?—built-light-for-flight bones,
Leached, bleached out, scaled to high kite zones—
Buoyance that scoured out, scored, then bored right, loans
Range to a flute floating our warm and bright tones
Over the vast frozen waste no man owns.

How far will you go for his hard, sharp toenails?—
For harp picks, guitar picks, to pick locks, open jails,
Thumb tacks, phononeedles, needles to sew sails,
To turn toward true North in high snowthrown trails
Or seek the soft South when winter winds blow gales.

For this heart, smart and artful, hey, where will you start?—
A life's thump pump, formed to pyrite love's feverchart!
Let's throw in lights, liver, lungs, each left, torn apart,
Worn out part. Who'll start out—shebang and applecart
Go along; so what's wrong? Who'll buy a heart?

> I, said the fly, I go for the eye.
> Me, said the beetle, I'll buy me a bone.
> Mine, said the earthworm, I take the heart.

Part II
Darkling

A Darkling Alphabet

A is for Atom, the source
of the matter. Within it,
childlike, primal forces
meet, pivoting their courses
as unlike poles attract, submit
to power's laws, commit
themselves to form and limit.
For good or evil, it,
like humans, can be split.

B is for Brain, which helps us cope,
sometimes, with theories, art,
math, cataclysms, styles,
passions and affections.
Its networked scope
and tally of connections
exceed the sum of all
particles in this universe.
There *are* imperfections:
all fall
short; some, apart;
its core is still a reptile's
and we don't know
what that rules. Still, it's the one hope
of human being. And the curse.
At birth, you *did* have one
with all its nerve cells, though
if you start
using it, new circuitries can grow.
With luck, that's scarcely just begun;
if it's done, we're done.

C is for Cow; when little, you
were told that she said, Moo,
and had a crumpled horn.
She could get in the corn
but breathed sweet timothy and clover.
Maybe she *has* jumped over
the moon only to reappear
in strange new guises here:
in plastic cartons, wax-
lined boxes, thin-sliced stacks
of cheese, ranked steaks or chops
lining cool butcher shops,
as catchers' mitts, chairs, shoes,
purses, things we use
each day. Still, it's curious how
you never see one now.

D is for Demand, which is
normally for power, riches,
privilege and freedom
(most likely freedom from,
not to). Also,
for some outward show
of earned respect and love
that other people know
lies far above
our merit, so
keep to themselves. Be mindful of
what rank, insatiable itches
fester in the britches
of those *other* lustful, greedy sons of bitches.

E is for Earth, the Earth
that each man gains at birth,
at death. He thinks his mirth
or grief, her wealth or dearth,
implicit with his worth.
She, meantime, spreads his berth.

F is for Family where
we first learn we must share
a world with others, bear
their being, spare, or care
for, what we want to drive
away. In its snug hive
we also learn to lie, connive,
blame, betray, and to survive.

G is for Glamour; once, that meant
a diabolical enchantment
gypsies or sorcerers could lay
over one's eyes; this took away
all common sense, all will to fight
their will, all care for wrong or right
until their power grew absolute.
Now'days, we'll take no substitute.

H is for Hitler, the great
purveyor of Glamour and of Hate
who promised heaven on earth, then tossed
us all to hell and holocaust
and fifty millions dead—a cost
that might seem small, suppose we'd lost.
Some who survived suspect
he hides among us still. Correct.
Their post-war histories
prove his victorious enemies
harbor him, in whole or part,
locked in the heart
of every living man or woman.
Hate this: he still is human.

I is for I, since we
are the only creatures whose Identity
concerns them. Most are content
to live; we must live with Intent.
We Invent Images, Ideas,
Ideals, are Impelled to be as
Important as our thought.
In time, we think we're what we're not.
Philosopher, teacher, poet
say you get one self: know it.
You just might grow it.

J is for Jay, whose splash
of gorgeousness transforms
middle class lawns—a slash
of blue-black plumes that clash
with business suits and sober norms
like school band uniforms.
Its music, sadly, is a brash,
rude jeer that well might waken
the dead—waken even critics, jurists—
pure poetry to purists
of the factory horn. Mistaken,
often, for American tourists.

K is for Key; we use
it to shut out a world that's rife
with possibilities we choose
to miss—murder, rape and theft,
e.g.   Jailed up inside our life,
we try to make terms with what's left:
three chairs that match, one wife.
It confers mastery of space
by setting bounds, is sovereign mace
and scepter to the exclusive place
where we think we belong.
It does as much for Song.

L is for Love, another
paradox. When we were born,
apparently our mother
fed us and so chose
to save our lives. Still, such care shows
our frailty. All our lives, we are torn
by our relentless needs
and our conspicuous scorn
for anything that feeds

and so betrays our weakness.
If that sounds like sickness,
think: we also admire and emulate
those we hate.

M is for Mystery that's never
scarce in this life. It will endure:
men are stone-blind; meantime, it winks
out everywhere. Yet each man thinks
there must be ways he can secure
its glance in favor of some clever
scheme or self-concerned endeavor.

Then these dolts boggle at our hurry
to find out what this world's about.
You've heard the Mystery-mongers say:
Wait! Wait! Mystery's being driven away!
Have faith: Mystery can look out
for itself—from all sides. Mystery
reads all the papers. Not to worry.

N is for Nest, that's hidden
far in the arched and bending limbs.
There, young boys are forbidden
to get too curious and molest
songbirds where they take their rest
or come together in unsuppressed
vaults of elation—as the blest
congregation of seraphim's
spanned cathedral groins attest
to exalted impulse and, possessed,
choir forth lascivious hymns.

O is for Others, the one
thing one can't abide. Comparison
is odious. We can't endure
that others seem stronger, more secure,
more gifted; self-preservation
and pride
drive out uncommon sense,
brilliance or power, try to dispense
with genius and its cruel pretense
to difference.
Lonely, bored, you take a bride
only in due time to learn
she has more concern
with some strange life of hers
than yours.
All men may be brothers;
brothers are known
for treachery. If you had your druthers
you'd just as lief be left alone
with your own
looking glass or clone.

P is for Power, whose name
has fallen into ill repute
since it corrupts—absolute
power, absolutely. Yet the same
thing must be said, also,
for weakness. All things can
corrupt those born corruptible: Man.
If you're gonna go, you're gonna go.
Further, we'd have to say
rich chances for increased fertility
lie, often, in impurity,
corruption and decay.
Rapists say if you can see
no possibility to escape
suffering or committing rape,
why not . . .? I don't think I'd agree.
It *might* pay to avoid hysterics
and broad theories. Offered powers,
free time, funds, you could manure flowers
or write yourself some deathless lyrics.

Q is for Quiet,
a deep calm in the ear
whose qualities allow the spirit
to seek out its own voice. You just might try it;
Quakers love it. Most others fear it
worse than the news they hear
of plague and riot.
Lord, won't you buy
us eight-tracks, horns for cars;
give us our daily fix of violence
from ghetto blasters, pitchmen; keep us high
while waiting for restoring silence
to settle among the stars
by and by.

R is for Rhythm, for the deep
push and pull of tides, the thud
of pulse and impulse in our blood
to rise and fall, wake and sleep,
the rhyme that beats time for the tune
and moves the circling sun and moon
waltzing around again to bring
summer, autumn, winter, spring
and renaissance to each green thing.
It's like a chime, the echoing sound
of heartbeat from our mothers' wombs
so all our lives we must surround
ourselves with music in our rooms.
We're like a relocated puppy
alone at night; if he wakes up, he
takes solace in the tick and talk
of an old, fur-wrapped alarm clock.
Failed musicians learn one fact:
true rhythms seldom are exact—
lovers, also, whose wild rhythm
propels them through a bestial dance
that moves their loins to take the chance
and unexpected children with them.

S is for Success
which we flee like a curse
and so dispossess
ourselves; some malediction which
we swore against the rich
could fall on our own head.
Then, too, one who succeeds
can't act abused or frail;
instead,
he must face others' needs.
We'd rather fail.
Yet this can make sense, too:
conquerors do well to do
with less
than everything. Choose
to win too much
too soon and you lose touch
with your wrongheadedness.
Lose
early and avoid the rush
at the war's end. Look up, perhaps,
the Avars or the Alans who
gained ground till they seemed ready to
swallow up all the maps;
now, nobody knows their name.
Species can do the same.

T is for Tyrant, one
who rules by force and terror,
deathsquad, noose and gun.
With no trial, no pity,
he'll rase field, farm and city
to sniff out every bearer
of bad news, all whose error
is thinking their own thoughts. If cursed
by those who live elsewhere
and can afford
such talk—who think their lord
more bountiful, much fairer,
tenderhearted—he should care.
By those who see him at his worst,
sweat cold beneath his sword,
he'll be adored.

U is for Urge
which we try to control;
still, even on the verge
of some long-sought goal,
we learn we've paid a toll:
we've had to purge
the surge
and voltage of our whole
self and soul.

V is for Vote. You do?
Supposing Whatchamacallit
And Whosis want to pick my wallet,
I don't pick who.

W is for Wrong which we,
however good or bright,
must be.
Dictators, hedged in might,
can wallow in one rare delight:
infallibility.
So, they prolong
the time before humanity
proves what mortal fools we be.
Achilles, strong,
self-righteous, racked with spite,
brought friend and foe alike to flight
and slaughter, yet in that great song,
bent his head, too, along
with the vast throng
of those who'd been, and who'd done, wrong.

X is for X-ray
that pries and pokes into
things set in its way.
Taking a broad view
of the body's blue-
prints, it can lay
out balance sheets
and schedules where it meets
our record of transactions, true
outlays and false receipts,
areas of decay
we're loath
to ponder, that dark growth
we hide away.
It discerns both
hairline splits in bone
and open, spikey
fractures. None is known
that witnesses the psyche.

Y is for Yes and that's
the poet's word. He must affirm
what makes ideacrats
and joiners itchy. He can't squirm

out by trying to deny
what doesn't fit his definition
of the Good and True. His mission
is to believe only his eye,

the burning witness of his senses,
his emotions, passions—
a private mandate that dispenses
with theories and fashions.

The rest all know how to create
a world they think would suit
them better, how to set life straight
by their lights, their law. He'd not dispute

one word, but sees the blind child starving
on the doorstep, bodies in the street
the rich drive down, lovers carving
each other's guts out, defeat

wrung from our greatest triumphs by
our greed and cowardice. He may
ask what and how and why;
he can't ask things to go away

unsaid. What he'd prefer
cuts no ice here. He knows his place is
breadth and his appetite embraces
victim and executioner.

His job's to celebrate
what IS—now, while it's not too late.
If all the groupies hate him,
he's doing *something* right; congratulate him.

Z is for Zero, the last
numeral and, in a blast,
the last place to be on the ground.
It's infinite, since round,
and devoid of any contrast.
All things on earth have passed,
or will, through this small, profound
hole to enter the vast
and the vacuum. It closes fast.

Disguised as Humpty-Dumpty,
W. D. Practices Tumbling

What is more odious than all
Fence-sitting, straddling a wall?
Why should we back away and stall
   Teetering here all day afraid of
   Showing the world the stuff we're made of?

We know a man by what he'll tumble
To; pride goes before a stumble.
It's falling keeps a body humble.
   Some fall to work, some to their meal;
   All life must fall with Fortune's wheel.

Some use their training and their talents
To walk up wires and keep their balance;
Some leap, all buoyancy and valiance,
   In broad air; still we judge their worth
   When they've come back in touch with earth.

Into the nest of twig and feather
The egg must fall; the question's whether
You bounce back keeping things together.
   Some fall to tumbling in the hay;
   Some fall in love and crack that way.

Let others practice wings and Springs;
The falling leaf, the fall of kings
Rings out the old—the downward swing
   Of clocks and stocks, the Fall of Man,
   Fall is where everything began.

We hope to build this to a smash
Hit sport just like the Fender Bash,
The Fall from Grace, the Market Crash.
    The real point isn't winning; what's
    Important is to show some guts.

The House the Poet Built

This is the house the poet built.

This is the silence everyone heard
Inside the house the poet built.

Here is the high goal out in the yard;
This is the silence everyone heard
Inside the house the poet built.

Here is a hummingbird on guard
Perched on the high goal out in the yard;
This is the silence everyone heard
Inside the house the poet built.

Here is the lady of his regard
Who watched the hummingbird standing guard
Next to the high goal in the yard;
This is the silence everyone heard
Inside the house the poet built.

Here are the heavens, many-starred,
Over the lady of his regard
Who saw the hummingbird on guard
Near to the high goal out in the yard;
This is the silence everyone heard
Inside the house the poet built.

Here is the hawk whose screams were heard
Throughout the heavens, many-starred,
Over the lady of his regard
Who saw the hummingbird stand guard
Near to the high goal out in the yard;
This is the silence everyone heard
Inside the house the poet built.

Here is the flitter-bat that whirred
At night when the hawk was no more heard
Under the heavens, many-starred,
Over the lady of his regard
Who knew where the hummingbird stood on guard
Beside the high goal out in the yard;
This is the silence everyone heard
Inside the house the poet built.

Here is the poet, the daft, old bard
Who watched the flitter-bats that whirred
At night when the hawk was no more heard
Under the heavens, radiant-starred,
Over the lady of his regard
Who fed the hummingbird standing guard
Beside the high goal out in the yard;
This is the silence everyone heard
Inside the house the poet built.

These are the lips that uttered the word
That rang in the ears of the dotty old bard
While watching the flitter-bats that whirred
At night when the hawk was no more heard
Under the heavens, radiant-starred,
That lit the lady of his regard
Who spoke to the hummingbird on guard
Beside the high goal in the yard;
This is the silence everyone heard
Clasped in the house the poet built.

Dostoievsky Warns W. D.
about Wearing Raskolnikov's Hat

(Dostoievsky, a large blue rabbit,
addresses a startled child.)

To step out sporting such a topper
Seems highfalutin' and improper
To men of average ability;
You catch their eyes, then their hostility.
They'll brand you uppity and vain,
Acting as if you had more brain
To cover up. You'll hear it said:
There's more inside this than his head—
What if he's smuggling contraband,
Cocaine or concealed weapons? *And*
There's room in such a tall hatband
For worse: a pair of rabbit ears!
He could be one of those that hears
Lost voices, taps top-secret thought
Whose meaning even we forgot,
That scans, like supersonic bats,
The blips we keep beneath our hats,
Decodes brain waves, bugs dreams of ours,
Broadcasting them to foreign powers!
Why else would he need such antennae?
Good honest folks sure don't have any.
Let's get rid quick of this high-hatted dude;
Besides, we just don't like his attitude.

W. D. Attempts to Swallow the Symbol' ' ' ' ' ' ' ' ' ' ' ' ' '

—The poet, assisted by a small
blue angel, tries to swallow a large
pyramidal object.

Never put anything, they tell you,
inside your ear
that's smaller than your elbow.
Then hand you THIS.
It is like swallowing your head
with corners. And, like a good deed
or an ill-intended oyster,
revisits you. It's
like a dumb love
song, this aftertaste
of doubt, of questioning
that says: too much yet not enough.
Here is this
triangle of equal sides and
Cajun dances, alarms
clanging, calls to prayer;
this trinitarian delta where
all waters ought
to flow; this pyramid
supposed to sharpen razors,
preserve our steaks and sanity,
restore time and your timepiece,
frame the God's eye and
my I.
With all the good will and with all
the orange juice in the world,

                                        it

won't

          go

down.

The Poet Ridiculed
by
Hysterical Academics

Is it, then, your opinion
    Women are putty in your hands?
Is this the face to launch upon
    A thousand one night stands?

First, please, would you be so kind
    As to define your contribution
To modern verse, the Western mind
    And human institutions?

        Where, where is the long, flowing hair,
           The velvet suit, the broad bow tie;
        Where is the other-worldly air,
           Where the abstracted eye?

Describe the influence on your verse
    Of Oscar Mudwarp's mighty line,
The theories of Susan Schmersch
    Or the spondee's decline.

        You've labored to present us with
           This mouse-sized volume; shall this equal
        The epic glories of Joe Smith?
           He's just brought out a sequel.

Where are the beard, the bongo drums,
Tattered T-shirt and grubby sandals,
As who, released from Iowa, comes
To tell of wondrous scandals?

Have you subversive, out of date,
Or controversial ideas?
And can you really pull your weight
Among such minds as these?

Ah, what avails the tenure race,
Ah, what the Ph.D.,
When all departments have a place
For nincompoops like thee?

Notes on Publication

I. *Heart's Needle* was first published by Alfred A. Knopf, Inc. in 1959. The following year the Marvell Press published an English edition which included a prose essay entitled "Finding a Poem". Of the original thirty poems, I here include seventeen.

II. *Remains* was first published in a small, letterpress edition under the pseudonym S. S. Gardons by the Perishable Press in 1970. After the death of my parents, a new edition was issued by BOA Editions, Ltd. under my own name. In that edition, as here, a single poem, "The Father", has been substantially revised.

III. *The Boy Made of Meat* was first written in 1962 for a series of children's books edited by Louis Untermeyer; it was accepted but never published since the series was discontinued. After Untermeyer's death William Ewert found the manuscript among Untermeyer's papers and asked if he could make a small, fine press edition. After substantial revisions in 1981 and 1982 it appeared in the latter year under his imprint.

IV. *After Experience* was first published by Harper & Row, Inc. in 1967; the following year, Oxford University Press issued an English edition. Of the forty poems I here include twenty-four. Of these, "Manet: 'The Execution of the Emperor Maximilian'" and "Van Gogh: 'The Starry Night'" have been substantially revised.

V. *The Fuehrer Bunker* was published as a "poem-in-progress" by BOA Editions, Ltd. in 1977. Two further selections from the cycle appeared in small, fine press edition: "Magda Goebbels" was published by Palaemon Press in 1983 and "Heinrich Himmler" by Pterodactyl Press in 1983. The cycle now consists of some seventy poems not including the choruses from the performance staged at The American Place Theatre in 1981 and from the performances at the University of Eastern Michigan at Ypsilanti, Michigan in 1987; I hope to finish it shortly. Of the sixteen poems included here, all but two appeared in the volumes listed above.

VI.   *If Birds Build with Your Hair* was published in a small letterpress edition by Nadja Press in 1979. I reprint here poems from that volume as well as one other poem written in the same period and never collected in a volume, "Coming Down from the Acropolis", which appeared as a separate broadside issued by the Derry Press.

VII.   *A Locked House* was published by William Ewert in 1986. I include here all poems from that volume as well as "D. D. Byrde Calling Jennie Wrenne", which was published by William Ewert in 1984.

VIII.   *Kinder Capers* is the title of a cycle of poems which includes as Part I "The Death of Cock Robin" and as Part II "Darkling". *The Kinder Capers,* published by Nadja Press in 1986, consisted of three poems included in this volume. A volume to be entitled *The Death of Cock Robin* will be published by The University of Delaware Press in 1987. That volume will contain thirty-three poems and reproductions of thirty-four paintings by DeLoss McGraw which often bear the same titles and to which the poems are intimately related. All the poems in *Kinder Capers* are closely related to paintings by DeLoss McGraw except "Through the Nursery Window". "Through the Nursery Window", which is dedicated to McGraw's son, is previously uncollected.